A CHAPTER *of the* HISTORY *of the* WAR *of* 1812 *in the* NORTHWEST

EMBRACING
THE SURRENDER OF THE
NORTHWESTERN ARMY AND FORT,
AT DETROIT, AUGUST 16, 1812

with a
Description and Biographical Sketch
OF THE
Celebrated Indian Chief Tecumseh

BY

Colonel William Stanley Hatch

Volunteer in the Cincinnati Light Infantry, and
from the invasion of Canada, to the surrender
of the Army, Acting Assistant Quartermaster General of that Army

HERITAGE BOOKS
2012

HERITAGE BOOKS
AN IMPRINT OF HERITAGE BOOKS, INC.

Books, CDs, and more—Worldwide

For our listing of thousands of titles see our website
at
www.HeritageBooks.com

A Facsimile Reprint
Published 2012 by
HERITAGE BOOKS, INC.
Publishing Division
100 Railroad Ave. #104
Westminster, Maryland 21157

Index Copyright © 2012 Heritage Books, Inc.

Entered, according to Act of Congress, in the year 1872,
by William Stanley Hatch
In the office of the Librarian of Congress at Washington

— Publisher's Notice —
In reprints such as this, it is often not possible to remove blemishes from the original. We feel the contents of this book warrant its reissue despite these blemishes and hope you will agree and read it with pleasure.
This book starts on page 5.

International Standard Book Numbers
Paperbound: 978-0-7884-2718-3
Clothbound: 978-0-7884-9165-8

INTRODUCTORY.

HISTORICAL INCIDENTS.

The aggressive acts of the British Government upon the ocean, especially in the boarding our merchant vessels, and forcibly taking therefrom any sailor that the boarding officer thought proper to consider as having been born in England, and forcing such of our citizens so taken into actual service on board their fleet, until the numbers taken reached nearly seven thousand, and this most insulting and hostile course having been continued for many years, notwithstanding the continued and earnest remonstrance of our Government, together with the instigation of the savage tribes of the west and north-west by English traders and the official agents of that Government to commit acts of hostility against our western settlements, had at length produced in the mind of almost every man west of the Alleghanies a feeling of hostility towards that Government, but by no means against the English people as individuals, as there were none of our citizens more respected or beloved, nor were there any more patriotic in volunteering in the war that ensued, than our fellow-citizens of English birth.

At the close of the Anglo-Indian war of 1791, the British Government still held, in contravention of the treaty of 1783, a strongly built fortress, near the foot of the Rapids of the Maumee, and which was persistently held by that Government for a length of time, and only vacated by British troops after many complaints and many remonstrances on the part of our Government. It was finally, after the close of this war by Wayne's treaty at Greenville of the third of August, 1795, evacuated, and our territory at that point was relieved of the presence of a hostile flag, and the forces of a foreign power, for so long a time trespassing upon our territory and instigating and assisting the savage tribes to continued hostility against our earliest settlers, in what was at that time a vast wilderness.

They however but crossed the head of the Lake to their previously established post of Malden, just at the entrance of the Detroit River into the Lake; and from this point they sought to keep a strong hold upon the Indian tribes of the old north-western territory as well as all others that they could reach or control. In carrying this policy into effect they made Malden their great trading post, and from it made to the Indians annually presents of arms and ammunition as well as medals, trinkets and showy articles of merchandise, and for the use and accommodation of this annual assembling of the Indian tribes, erected a large Council House, and established their great council ground at *Brownstown*, near to Lake Erie, and within our territory of Michigan. Again by this act of flagrant aggression upon our territory, continuing the bitter feeling manifested towards us on every occasion.

These annual convocations of all the Indian tribes of the north-west were attended by British agents, speaking their language, or haranguing them through their interpreters.

It was here that Elliot and McKee, two most atrocious renegades from the United States, whose presence at St. Clair's defeat was made known to us after the treaty of Greenville by Indian chiefs, who asserted that they, especially the latter, tomahawked more of our soldiers, and tore the scalps from more of our wounded men than any Indian actor in that terrible conflict. It was here that these men with bloody hands and scalps of American citizens ornamenting their dress, regularly met the Indians in council, speaking their language, and as chief agents of the British Government with royal commissions as British officers, had immense influence over them.

In the meantime TECUMSEH and his brothers had grown up to manhood, and whilst one of them became renowned throughout all the north-west and south-west as a mighty PROPHET of the GREAT SPIRIT, one other became the WARRIOR and GREAT ORATOR of his tribe and race. They unitedly matured their great plan for a general confederation of all the Indian tribes to act and war against any further approach and dominion of the WHITE RACE, and if possible to regain their old territorial boundary of the Ohio River.

Large bodies of Indians were gathered at different points. The PROPHET was ever busy teaching them and promising a glorious future when they should have "*driven the white race back to the ocean from whence they came*,"* which the Great Spirit had said to him, should be done if they

---

*The "PROPHET" re-produced these great words: "*drive the white race back to the ocean from whence they came*," which had been the rallying cry of the great "PONTIAC," a half a century before. This he did as giving higher promises from the favor of the GREAT SPIRIT in their behalf than what TECUMSEH or the chiefs of the great tribes contended for or expected, even in the event of the greatest success.

They hoped to regain their old boundary, the Ohio River. In this they were consistent: they had contended for it in the War of 1791, and when our government endeavored after Harmar's and St. Clair's defeats, and before Wayne's campaign, to make peace with them, they unitedly refused, except upon the terms of this boundary; and our Government during its negotiations with them had to put in the plea, that, as by the treaty of "FORT HARMAR" a part of the territory had been ceded to the United States, and *already partially occupied in good faith*, the old limits could not be agreed too, but that the then existing limits and boundaries should forever be held sacred and inviolate. British officers and agents had promised them in 1791, if they would make a general war on the American settlements already established in the north-western territory, that all the power and all the warriors of the king of Great Britain, their great father beyond the rising sun, should be brought to their support, and would certainly secure to them forever the boundary of the Ohio River.

would obey his word and unite with a determined will in support of the great cause.

At the same time TECUMSEH was actively engaged in visiting, accompanied by a chosen band of young warriors, every Indian tribe from Lake Superior on the north, to Florida in the south, and holding councils with them, and urging with his vehement oratory that general combined action so necessary to ensure the success of their great effort in a universal war

The summer of 1811 arrived, when the government deemed it necessary to bring a large force into the field to meet and put down this dangerous combination.

The old 4th regiment of Infantry, raised and officered mostly in New Hampshire and Massachusetts, and commanded by Colonel Boyd, was ordered to report at Vincennes, to General William Henry Harrison, then Governor of the Indiana Territory. At the same time several regiments of volunteer mounted Infantry were called for from the

State of Kentucky, and marched in the months of September and October to the same post.

These forces under the command of Governor Harrison, advanced up the line of the Wabash; established the post of Fort Harrison; moved on, and on the sixth of November, in the afternoon, encamped on rising ground near Tippecanoe Creek, having an extensive prairie just in front, and the Indian village known as the PROPHET'S TOWN, being the main point for which the army marched, a short distance in advance. It was here that the Indians had been assembled for several months, and were then known to be in large force. Yet Governor Harrison did not expect that they would attack him, but that on seeing his large and well appointed army, would for the time at least pretend a disposition for peace, and gradually disperse to their villages or tribes. In this, however, he was mistaken, as at 4 o'clock the next morning they made their attack. It was impetuous, and in great force, and made almost simultaneously on both flanks and the rear of the camp, first breaking through the pickets, with silent approach creeping upon the earth through the tall grass, slaying nearly all. They then rushed with great fury through and over the main guards, and entered the camp amidst the tents of our troops, with terrific yells.

It required all the coolness and bravery of the troops to repel them, which they did, so soon as they were up and formed in line; not, however, until many of our brave and distinguished officers and men had fallen. One hundred and eighty-eight men and officers killed and wounded, was the resulting loss on our part; and about an equal number of Indians killed, and probably an equal number wounded, was the amount of the Indian loss, in what was in fact the first battle of the war, publicly declared in the following year, and known in history as the war of 1812.

The battle of Tippecanoe was fought.

This was on the morning of the seventh of November, 1811.

The Kentucky Volunteers returned home. The 4th U. S. regiment was stationed at Fort Harrison and Vincennes until the month of May, 1812, when it marched for Ohio, and joined the north-western army, then fully organized, and having moved forward from the plains of Mad River, was encamped at Urbana, Champaign county, and the commanding officer was holding a council with the chiefs of the Wyandott, Ottoway, Miami, and other Indian tribes living within the boundaries of the State of Ohio, for a peaceful passage of the army through the Indian territory, commencing a few miles north of Urbana, and extending with few exceptions to Detroit.

The imminence of war with Great Britain had become so great that in the winter of

1811 and 1812, the general government deemed it necessary that a body of volunteers should be called for from the State of Ohio, to march on the opening of the season northward to Detroit, in order that this then remote frontier post should in all events be well protected, and in the event of war being declared, be in readiness to move promptly upon upper Canada.

THREE FULL REGIMENTS were called for, and the men composing this force PROMPTLY RESPONDED to the call. They marched in detachments from the southern, the central, and the south-eastern parts of the State, under the direction of Governor Meigs, for the plains of Mad River, three miles above Dayton, there to choose field officers and fully organize.

Brigadier-General William Hull, then Governor of the Territory of Michigan, arrived from Washington City with his aids-de-camp, Captain Hickman and Captain

Abraham F. Hull his son,* on the 22nd of April, 1812, and established his headquarters at the COLUMBIAN INN, at the south-west corner of Main and Second streets, Cincinnati, then the principal tavern in the town; and during the last of April and first week of May, made his arrangements for the necessary supplies and transportation of the army. He then proceeded on to Dayton, and superintended the organization of the Ohio volunteers; and having completed his arrangements, in the last week of May commenced his line of march for Detroit, as commander in chief of the north-western army, as it was now styled.

---

* Captain Hull, afterwards, at the desperately contested and bloody battle of Lundy's Lane, on the 25th day of July, 1814, gallantly fell at the head of his command in the *last charge of the enemy,* just as the *moon was setting* at *eleven o'clock at night;* and is buried where he fell, in the little graveyard on the crest of the ridge, then occupied with a battery, which four hours previous had been so gallantly carried by Colonel Miller of our old 4th, then of the 21st regiment.

He had become old and *quite fat*, and had evidently lost the energy as well as the valor, that thirty-three years previous had given him the post of honor with ANTHONY WAYNE, in carrying the fortress of Stony Point.

The Cincinnati Light Infantry with which I was connected, was commanded by

Captain, JOHN F. MANSFIELD, a gentleman and a soldier

Lieutenant, STEPHEN McFARLAND, a good and generous hearted man.

Ensign, THOMAS HECKEWELDER, a merchant and an excellent man.

Orderly Sergeant, JAMES CHAMBERS, a well known and esteemed citizen.

The members of the company were young men, merchants, artizans, and tradesmen, all of the highest respectability.

This company was at the organization of the army attached to the 3d regiment, instead of the 2nd, which was composed of volunteers from Hamilton, Warren, and other conterminous counties in the southwestern part of Ohio.

It marched for Dayton, together with several companies of the 2nd regiment, on the 14th of May.

As before stated, the army halted at Urbana, and the commanding general held a council with the Indians through whose territories it had to march to reach Detroit. Their assent was given with apparent and averred friendly feelings; no opposition was encountered; the weather was warm and pleasant. The dense forest extending with but few exceptions, the entire distance, furnished shade in day time and shelter at night.

The marches were easy, as a wagon trace had to be opened, and block-houses as posts had to be built at several points. The army passed through the wilds of Ohio, reaching and crossing the Maumee River at the foot of the rapids in fine health, on the 30th of June; and on the 3rd day of July first heard of the DECLARATION OF WAR, which had been made on the 18th of June.

DECLARATION OF WAR!

THE ARMY REACHES DETROIT.

INVASION OF CANADA.

July 3, 1812.—At 2 o'clock, p. m., whilst under march, near the River Raisin, we received dispatches from Washington City, announcing the Declaration of War against England. The late Judge Shaler, of Pittsburgh, then a young man, was the bearer of the dispatches.

During the forenoon of Saturday, the 4th of July, the army reached the River Huron, after passing some miles through a heavily timbered swamp. The river where struck was deep, with the water near the surface of the ground; banks perpendicular, width perhaps fifty or sixty feet. A floating bridge, made of the timber of the vicinity, and transported by a large fatigue force, was constructed in a short time; so that the entire army, with all the baggage and stores, was passed over the river before sunset. We bivouacked in the prairie in front; the grass in which was then at an average height of about three feet.

JULY 5th.—The army passed the Indian council ground at Brownstown, crossed the River *Rouge*,* advanced and encamped at "*Spring Wells*," estimated at that time to be from three to four miles from the Fort of Detroit.

JULY 6th.—Monday, the Fourth Regi-

---

* This river was then called the *Rouge* by Americans, and by most of the French; and the *E'course* by other French inhabitants, from the fact that their ancestors had obtained, from along its banks, the *bark of trees* in large quantities, for the covering of their rude dwellings at the period of their earliest settlement, transporting it by their bateaux and canoes to the shore of Detroit. (The strait).

ment U. S. Infantry marched to the fort, and occupied it.

JULY 7th.—The volunteers marched, and took position near the fort on the south, west and north. Arrangements were now made by procuring a large supply of bateaux to move on Canada.

JULY 8th.—Orders were issued for the army to be in readiness to march and cross the river at 2 o'clock the next morning.

JULY 9th.—This morning at 2 o'clock, A. M., the army moved up the bank of the river in the following order:

1. The Fourth U. S. Regiment, Lieutenant Colonel James Miller.
2. The First Regiment Ohio Volunteers, Colonel Duncan McArthur.
3. The Second Regiment Ohio Volunteers, Colonel James Findlay.
4. The Third Regiment Ohio Volunteers, Colonel Lewis Cass.

The advance column reached a point parallel to the lower end of the island (then called Hog Island or Isle Descochon), the columns wheeled by the right into line, by which movement the Third Regiment volunteers became the right of the army.

It was now daylight of a delightful bright summer morning. The whole line entered bateaux, which had on the preceding evening been taken from opposite the fort, down the river, to a point opposite Sandwich, in order to mislead the enemy as to the place selected for our advance, and had been brought back to this point after 12 o'clock.

The Cincinnati Light Infantry were on the extreme right. We, together with Captain Mansfield, Orderly James Chambers, the late Elias Sayre, John Highway, John Lawrence, and others entered the bateaux furthest down the river. These bateaux were a class of boats used by the Canadians in their voyages on the lakes, and as traders carrying their stores. They had no deck; were merely large skiffs.

The flotilla proceeded very regularly and handsomely dressed in line, the right a little in advance. Standing in the bow with Captain Mansfield, in looking to the left, we could see every boat, and distinguish each regiment. On passing the middle of the river, our wing gradually gained further in advance; and as our Captain was very watchful as we neared the shore, lest some on our left should push ahead out of line, in order to gain the shore before us, he gave orders in an undertone to the oarsmen to give headway. The result was, we struck shore more than a rod in advance of any other boat, and our company had landed and formed in column as the head of the advance, before the center and left had reached the shore

We were not attacked on landing, as we had expected. Oblique to the right, and on a bluff quite near to where we landed, was a strongly built mill (it was still standing in 1856 the last time I was in Detroit), and we thought it more than probable that our enemy, who is ever ready for a fight in time of war, had placed and masked a light battery within it, which, with their sharpshooters, might annoy us considerably before our advance in force would have caused their precipitate retreat. But we met with no resistance.

We marched down the road along the bank of the river, to a point opposite the town, presenting a fine appearance from the opposite shore, according to the description of those who witnessed it. The inhabitants (nearly all Canadian French) welcomed us as friends. White handkerchiefs and flags waved from every house, and the expression, "We like the Americans," came forth from every dwelling.

A vacant, unfinished two story brick house, still standing in 1856, belonging, it was said, to a Colonel Babie, with extensive grounds, became the head quarters and entrenched camp of the north - western army in Canada. The roof of the house was shingled, the floors laid, and the windows in; otherwise it was entirely unfinished. A partition of rough boards was put up on each side of the hall, which ran entirely through the house. General Hull, with his aids, occupied the north half of the house. General James Taylor, late of Newport, Kentucky, Quarter Master General of the army, with his two assistants, occupied the south side. The entrance to the hall and its use was common to both. The councils of war were held in the second story, over the room occupied by the commanding General, access to which was had by a rough stairway. A free and unrestricted, confidential intercourse existed. Everything was known to us. Each day's events and incidents were freely communicated. General Hull and his son, Captain Hull, lodged most of the time at head quarters. General Taylor, being unwell, lodged in Detroit. Major Taylor Berry,

Assistant Quarter Master General, and myself, attended to the duties of our office every day, and lodged in it every night, except a few nights when I was out on reconnoisances with the troops.

I state these facts with more particularity, in order to show that my official position of acting Assistant Quarter Master General of the army, and my unrestricted personal intercourse with the officers at head-quarters, gave me all the facilities which could be desired for obtaining correct information on every point. And I may further state that in accepting the appointment, I reserved the right to join my company whenever ordered on duty beyond the camp, in which a reconnoisance of the enemy's position or an advance upon his lines, might lead to a conflict with him or his allies, the Indians.

Here the army lay for four weeks, during which time a detachment under the command of Colonel McArthur marched up the River Thames, and returned with large supplies of flour, wheat, beef cattle, and between eight hundred and a thousand sheep. The latter were all sent over the river, and ranged at large on the extensive common back of the Fort, and there remained until after the surrender of the army, when I saw the Indians busy killing them, and appropriating the fine mutton they afforded to their use.

A reconnoisance in force under the command of Colonels McArthur and Cass, marched to the vicinity of Malden, carrying the enemy's battery posted at the bridge over the Canard River, 14 miles from our camp, and 4 miles above Malden. Another reconnoisance by the Light Infantry and a small detachment of the 4th U. S. regiment commanded by Captain Snelling, was made about the 20th of July, by which it was ascertained that the enemy had withdrawn his out post at the "Canard" bridge, and had stationed the Queen Charlotte off and near the mouth of the Canard River, in position of observation.

Another movement was then planned by the same officers and others, to construct some floating batteries, place a 24 pound gun upon each, and with the addition of a few gunners and sailors, then in Detroit, to descend along the shore of the river on the first dark night, and board the Queen Charlotte, and from her deck call on the commanding general to march the army and enter Malden. This project was not sanctioned at head-quarters, and all that could be obtained was permission to make a further reconnoisance, and ascertain the precise position of this vessel. In making this reconnoisance it was intended if possible to carry her by boarding; but the attempt, for the want of the batteries and sailors, did not succeed, particularly as the night brightened after 12 o'clock, so as to discover us to the enemy too soon. At this time the enemy had posted a small Indian force on the line of our communication with the State of Ohio, and had captured the bearer of despatches from head-quarters as well as private correspondence, which of course were taken to Malden. General Hull therefore ordered Major Vanhorne, of the 2nd regiment volunteers, with two companies of Infantry, a part of a company of volunteer cavalry, together with a part of a company of rifles, to escort the mail and despatches, as well as a few gentlemen belonging to the commissary department returning to Ohio.

He proceeded down the same road the army had marched up on its approach to Detroit, and on reaching a point nearly opposite Malden, about the centre of Gros Isle, well selected for the purpose by the Indians, was attacked, and after the loss of some brave men and officers, compelled to make a precipitate retreat back to the Fort. This little discomfiture, together with the reception at head-quarters of information that Fort Mackinac had been captured by the enemy, appeared to have alarmed the commanding general, and to have divested him of all self possession or control over his fears.

From the 20th July, the army was in daily expectation of orders to march on Malden. The enemy's weakness was well known.

As General Hull, in his endeavors to extenuate the act of his surrender, alleges, among other causes, the want of subsistence for his army, I will here state that on a morning early in August, whilst in conversation with one of his Aids, at the front door of head-quarters, a respectable looking man was passed in through the guard, approached, and said he wished to see General Hull. The Aid informed the General, who walked to the door, when the person, after salutation, said, "*General*, as your chief commissary is absent, I have taken the liberty of calling and saying that I have one hundred head of cattle, which

I can deliver in a day or two." General Hull replied, "I do not want them; I have plenty;" turned and walked into his quarters.

On the evening of the 7th August, it was reported in camp that the army would march on MALDEN during the night and early in the morning. At 11 o'clock tents were struck and loaded, and the wagon train was moving; but instead of moving down the road, in the direction of Malden, was driven to the landing, and taken by ferry boats across the river, and stationed on the common, north of the fort.

Orders were issued during the night to break up camp, and recross the river to Detroit!

The most profound astonishment and indignation, at what was felt as a disgrace, pervaded the army.

The opinion universally prevailed, and was openly expressed by officers and men, that the Commanding General had committed an unpardonable and fatal error in not having marched the army upon Malden, to which he was repeatedly and earnestly urged, to my personal knowledge, when the extreme weakness of the enemy was well ascertained by our reconnoisances and secret service, fully confirmed by deserters coming into head-quarters every morning. His force having been reduced by desertion from six hundred and sixty Canadian militia to one hundred and sixty; from one hundred Indians under Tecumseh to sixty, and having but two hundred and twenty-five regulars; it was also known that the British officers had already sent their most valuable effects on board their vessels in the port, preparatory to a precipitate evacuation of the post. Yet no one, except those near the Commanding General, had the most distant idea that he had thought of giving up the post of Detroit, or surrendering the army; a post which could not have been taken by any force the enemy could have brought against it; and an army with an abundance of subsistence; at this time, according to the official report of the Brigade Major, acting as Adjutant General of the army, numbering 2,300 effective men, well supplied with artillery, independent of the guns of the fort and advanced batteries.

On the 9th of August, a strong detachment was marched down the road, with orders to attack the enemy who had crossed from Malden in force, and taken up a position nearly opposite the center of Gros Isle, cutting our communication with Ohio. The detachment reached them at 3 o'clock, P. M.; immediately charged upon their lines, and drove them three miles to their boats, when, as it had become dark and raining, the most of them escaped to Malden.

In this action the numbers on each side were about equal. The British brought into the field a large part of their regulars, together with all the Indian force, the whole under the command of Major Muir. Our attack upon their position, which was strengthened by temporary breast works, formed of logs and fallen trees, was dashing and entirely successful.

The communication with Ohio was opened, and the enemy defeated. The next day the detachment, after sending forward the mails and dispatches, returned to the fort. Our loss was rather larger than that of the enemy (sixty-eight men), as the Indians had the first fire from behind their logs and trees; they were prevented, however, by our charge and pursuit, from having another. This action was known in the army as the battle of *Magauga*, about fourteen miles below Detroit; it was afterward known as the battle of Brownstown.

We here met a very great increase of Indian force which had recently joined the standard of Tecumseh, who, as we ascertained a few days afterward, had, on the receipt of intelligence of the fall of Mackinac, dispatched his runners to all his associate tribes to assemble at Malden immediately; that the fort at Mackinac had been taken by the British forces; that the American army had shown, by not marching on Malden, and by the easy discomfiture of several detachments, that they would not fight; that the braves should come forward with all speed, so as to participate in the capture of the army, and share in the plunder, which would be great. His appeal was promptly responded to. So that instead of but sixty men under his command, as so lately had been the case, he now had nearly six hundred; and by the 16th seven hundred warriors had joined him, who, as a body, were probably never equalled; certainly never excelled in the annals of Indian warfare. They were noble specimens of their race.

A suspicion strongly grounded and deeply felt on the part of the most active and intelligent of the volunteers, had now risen to such a point, that there was no longer any confidence reposed in the valor or patriotism of the Commanding General. A consultation was held, and it was decided to get up a Round Robin, as it was called, addressed to the three Colonels of the Ohio Volunteers, requesting the arrest or displacement of the General, and devolving the command on the eldest of the Colonels, McArthur. This was on the 12th of August.

On the following day it was reported that an armistice, or at least a temporary cessation of hostilities, had been agreed upon by the British authorities, and our armies on the Niagara and northern frontier, and that Major General Brock, Governor of Upper Canada, an officer of high reputation, had arrived at Malden to conduct their operations in this quarter.

The suspicion and distrust of the army was increased by General Hull's peremptory refusal to allow that distinguished officer, Captain, afterwards Colonel Snelling, (after earnest and repeated solicitation) to cross the river in the night, to carry and destroy an unfinished battery, which was being constructed from the cellar of a house on the opposite bank, and close to it, under the direction of Captain Dixon of the royal artillery.* This was the only battery of any consequence established by the enemy, and the only one that injured us. It opened on the afternoon of the 15th, and continued its cannonade during the morning of the 16th, when one of its balls struck and in-

---

*Captain Dixon was afterwards taken prisoner at the attack of Fort Stevenson; he narrowly escaped death at the time, and only escaped, as he informed me, by being in the act of leaping the ditch at the moment of the deadly discharge of the cannon from the little block-house bastion, at the south-west angle of the Fort, the balls and grape passing under his feet, and killing every man who had entered *the ditch* in making the assault. This discharge of a single cannon, (and they had but one,) directed for the moment by the gallant Croghan in person, literally filling the ditch with the slain, with the simultaneous fall of Colonel Short their commander, repulsed the enemy.

stantly killed Lieutenant Hanks, who had been in command at Mackinac, was then a prisoner of war on parole, the vessel in which himself and command had been sent down from Mackinac having been brought to by our water battery. The British journals did great injustice to this officer by asserting that he, when killed, was in the Fort as a combatant, breaking his parole; when in truth he had but called to see an army friend of his, and was standing in the gorge of the north-east bastion in conversation with him when struck by the ball. The same ball passed on and mortally wounded Surgeon Reynolds of the third regiment volunteers, by taking off both legs above the knee.

Thursday, August 13th, arrived. It had now become absolutely necessary that the greatest vigilance should be maintained by our guards, and that the outlying pickets should be greatly increased.

The Brig Adams, built and just repaired

at the mouth of the river Rouge, had been towed up by a party under the command of Captain Kyle, of Clermont county. She had her masts and spars, but not her sails or armament, and was anchored in the river just above the foot of the street running down by Smith's Tavern. On this evening (13th) the guard on this vessel was enjoined to observe especial watchfulness, lest the enemy should attempt under cover of the darkness of the night to cut her out. And in addition to the usual guard on deck, a small bateau with men was stationed at her bow, and another at her stern, whilst the officer in command occasionally visited each in a small bark canoe propelled without noise. At eleven o'clock, on placing the ear close to the surface of the water, the sound of quick, though precise stroke of oars was heard, the sound became more distinct, and there was soon seen by the dim starlight a small bateau rapidly approaching the landing at the foot of the street, containing two men at the oars, and two sitting aft. On being challenged, the boat came up, and one of the gentlemen gave the word and countersign. He was well known, and known to have the confidence of the commanding general more than any other officer, and in almost every instance had been entrusted with the duty of intercourse by flag, with the enemy. The other gentleman appeared, as near as could be judged by the dim light, to be young, well formed, of military bearing, and as they both left the bateau and walked up from shore, seemed rather taller than his companion. They directed their steps to the head-quarters of the commanding general and entered it, remaining three hours; they then returned to the boat, crossed to the Canadian shore; the boat came back; one of the gentlemen only was in her. He gave the word and passed on.

At that time, on that night, the capitulation of the Fort and surrender of the northwestern army was agreed upon. The parties to that agreement were General Hull, and on the part of the British, Major Glegg, one of the aids-de-camp of General Brock.

This is a historic fact which Major Glegg, if alive will corroborate, as after the war in 1815, at a hotel in Philadelphia, he communicated his participation in the act as above stated to the late quarter-master general of the north-western army, General James Taylor, of Newport, Ky.

Previous to this time a reinforcement, as was stated of two hundred and thirty men under the command of Colonel Henry Brush, of Chillicothe, Ohio, convoying supplies, including one hundred head of cattle, had arrived at the little French settlement, known as French town, at the crossing of the River Raisin, thirty-five miles from the Fort. Here they halted in consequence of the threatening attitude of the enemy, and reported to the commanding general. Common military conduct would seem to indicate the marching of such part of the army as would in any emergency be equal to any effort of the enemy, in the direction of these supplies, and on the nearest route down the main road until they were met, and then of conducting them to the Fort, giving the enemy battle, whenever and wherever he should make his appearance.

This was the expectation of the army; but contrary to this, orders were issued from head quarters on the afternoon of Friday, the 14th of August, for a detachment of about 360 men, under the command of the Colonels of the first and third regiments of Ohio Volunteers, the former acting as senior officer, with directions to march at twilight on the line of a circuitous route or trail, which passed by the river Rouge, several miles above its mouth, and continued far into the interior, passing the Huron, and striking the Raisin, passed down that stream or near it, to French Town. Accompanying the order was a message to the Colonels, that Colonel Brush had been ordered to move from his

HISTORY OF THE WAR OF 1812. 47

camp up this route, and would doubtless be met between the Rouge and the Huron, and at a distance not exceeding twelve miles from the Fort; but if he should not have advanced so far, the detachment would continue its march until he was met. The officers of the detachment believing that they would meet Colonel Brush and party, and return with it to Detroit by two or three o'clock A. M., and desiring the troops to march light and rapid, directed that no food or baggage be taken along, not even their blankets, nor would they detain for supper.

This order at the time excited no particular suspicion. The course adopted was attributed to timidity, over-ruling sagacious and prompt military conduct on the part of the commanding general. But here all were deceived, as *no order had been sent to Colonel Brush, to move in the direction stated, or to move at all.*

The sole object of the movement was to reduce the active force at the Fort, preliminary to carrying into effect the capitulation which had already been agreed upon, to get rid of a large number of officers and men known to be keenly sensitive to an honorable success, and had been openly hostile to the inaction of the army when in Canada, and to the recrossing the river, and who, if present, would unquestionably have resisted to the extremest point, regardless of all or any consequences, any attempt to surrender the Fort or the army.

The detachment marched at dusk, crossing the common directly in the rear of the Fort westward for near a mile, entered the forest and followed a path which at length intersected the road leading from Spring Wells to a small settlement of two hewed log two-story houses with gardens enclosed by split paling fence, which stood near the bank of the river Rouge. The wagon road passed in front of these houses and along the bank of the river for a considerable distance. Here the detachment halted, seven miles from the Fort by the road. At this point looking down the course of the stream, I saw at a bend of the river, apparently a quarter of a mile distant, a single horseman, the bright starlight revealing his figure against the dense foliage around him. Struck by the object, I turned to my friend Captain Mansfield, of the Cincinnati Light Infantry, to direct his attention to it, but before he could catch the view the horseman wheeled and disappeared.

As it was possible there might be a mistake in this, that it might be an optical delusion, we made no mention of it till long afterwards, when we had read General Brock's account of the capture of the Fort and army, contained in his despatches to his government (not the account as published in Niles Register), in which, after stating his arrangements for his intended attack, says, that *he was more especially induced to an immediate attack in consequence of his scout* having brought in the information *on the night of the 14th, that a large detachment of the enemy had been seen under march, three mile in the rear of the point selected for his landing.*

He landed near Spring Wells on the morning of the 16th, at which time his scouts had brought him the intelligence that this detachment was *on the preceding evening* (15th), *thirty-eight miles in his rear.*

This official statement of General Brock completely solved all doubts or mystery in regard to the preconcerted arrangement for a capitulation, and elucidated the plan by which General Hull carried it into effect, which he had evidently contemplated prior to the re-crossing the river, and had fully determined on, and arranged with Major Glegg, acting for General Brock, three days previous.

The detachment moved on five miles further to the point at which Colonel Brush was to have been met. We neither saw or heard anything of him, and after a halt of some hours, at 2 o'clock A. M. of 15th, continued the march, crossed the Huron at the ford, water waist deep, nothing but a trail through the forest, marched without again halting until 4 o'clock P. M. having reached the upper waters of the Raisin. Here the detachment halted and a part of a troop of horse was sent forward, down along the route to within twelve miles of the settlement of French Town. They returned at 6 o'clock P. M. and reported no sign of Colonel Brush. He had evidently not left his camp. The detachment being now from thirty-five to forty miles from Detroit, commenced its return march; a suspicion flashed across the mind of many that something disastrous was to occur; though even yet no one suspected the commanding general of an arranged plan for a capitulation. It halted for an hour at 1 o'clock A. M. on the 16th, and then proceeded. At the first dawn of day, cannonading was heard in the direction of the Fort; which continued at times with considerable briskness, till about 10 o'clock, when it ceased; from which we judged that the enemy had crossed the river below the town, had marched up, made an attack, and *of course* having been repulsed, had retreated.

If the firing had continued until the detachment had reached the little settlement on the river Rouge, it would have entered by the Spring Wells road, and have come in on the left flank and rear of the enemy, and doubtless as we believed, would have captured the entire of the British forces, as they would have been between the fires of our volunteers in front of the Fort and ours in their rear. The Indians would have given way as soon as charged upon with the bayonet, as they had at the action at Maguaga or Brownstown, and as they always have done.

Entertaining these exhilarating hopes, although without food for so long a time,

HISTORY OF THE WAR OF 1812. 53

the troops composing this detachment without exception appeared stimulated by the anticipated and hoped for conflict, and rejoiced in the expectation of achieving a fine affair, and having after all satisfaction for their hard tramp. With these high and cheering expectations they not only marched in double quick time, but actually kept up with the slow trot of the horse for at least twenty miles, when the cannonade having ceased, they resumed their usual march, and without once halting, until they arrived at about 1 o'clock P. M. at the edge of the woods which we had entered two nights before; when to our utter astonishment and indignation we beheld the BRITISH FLAG floating from the flag staff of the Fort, and the Indians in the extensive common before us busy taking horses and cattle.

The FORT of DETROIT and the NORTH-WESTERN ARMY had been SURRENDERED! Our detachment as we soon learned, and even Colonel Brush at the River Raisin were included. Colonel Brush, however, decided that he would not be surrendered. He detained the British Flag sent to inform him of the capitulation, in polite duress only long enough to give his good fellows with their hundred beeves a good start for Ohio, where they all arrived safely.

Here we may pause to record some of the momentous consequences of this most disastrous and infamous act, the surrender of a numerous and well appointed army, with a strong fortress.

The whole country was dishonored! The Volunteers of Ohio, composed of the élite of the State, young men of energy, talent and patriotism, many of whom in after life became her governors, legislators, senators and representatives in congress, and not only established and directed her civil destinies, but also gave to territories of the union their highest officers, and to the general government some of her ablest representatives abroad and statesmen at home. They were dishonored, and their State was dishonored. Truly the "weapons of war were vilely cast away," not by those who, with brave minds and quick hands, would have wielded them to the destruction of their country's enemies, but by him, who, as a national calamity, and a scourge upon a brave people and a righteous cause, had been, in a fatal hour, appointed to their chief command.

And above and beyond all this, the entire northwestern frontier was thus uncovered. The Indians far and near, with a few tribal exceptions, now joined as British allies in the war. All the evils arising from a great Indian war upon an extended frontier; all the blood shed at the massacre at FORT DEARBORN; at the *defeat of Winchester* on the *river Raisin;* at the *defense* of FORT MEIGS; at the *defeat* and *capture* of *Dudley's Regiment* at the *Maumee;* and during the protracted continuance of active hostilities throughout the northwest, with the great loss of life, independent of the slain, together with the immense national expense incident thereto, from this day up to the battle of the Thames, were the fatal results of this most disastrous act; an act apparently so little appreciated or comprehended as to its consequences by the Commanding General at the time, that he, evidently under the influence of extreme timidity, rather than encounter the enemy and achieve an important advantage by marching upon Malden and occupying that important post, to which he was so strongly urged, sank into the most lamentable condition of imbecility. This or treason can alone account for his conduct, and a merciful feeling, as well as a mature judgment, points to the former rather than to the latter as the over-ruling cause, on his part.

In order that those who come after us, and shall occupy the domain of the old northwestern Territory, at a period of time when, by the acts of civilized man, there shall no longer be a wilderness, or an Indian tribe within its vast limits, may the better comprehend the condition of our country at this time, I may state that only the eastern and southern parts of Ohio were settled, and that even these portions of the State were but thinly peopled. By drawing a line from near Cleveland on Lake Erie, to the falls of the Ohio River, all north and west of that line, with the exception of a few old French posts, with their feeble settlements, was, as it respects our race, an unbroken wilderness, an untouched forest, occupied by powerful Indian tribes, with no other defences than what the feeble stockade posts, known as the Forts Wayne, Dearborn, Harrison and the really strong fort of Detroit afforded. This fort, constructed according to the plan of the most skillful engineers, situated as it was, to command and control the great center of Indian power, a most important position from which to move on and control

Upper Canada; a safeguard and protection to our frontier settlements during the continuance of the war, so important to us in every respect, *should have been maintained above all others*, at every *hazard* and at every *sacrifice*. This was the judgment, and this was the feeling of every intelligent man in the northwestern army.

We recur to our subject: The detachment of the army, whose movements we are narrating, on viewing the enemy's flag floating from the fort, and with a glance of the eye, seeing that there could be no recovery; that the deed was fully done, had no course left but to countermarch to the River Rouge, and taking position in the two vacated log houses and gardens before mentioned, proceed to deliberate upon the course best to be adopted under the then existing circumstances. They had to take into consideration

First. That the troops had already been

under march for two days and two nights without any subsistence.

Second. That it would require a further march of from forty to fifty miles to arrive at Col. Brush's encampment, where subsistence could be had. And it was extremely doubtful whether we should find him there, as the enemy after the capitulation could detach the greater part of his Indian and some of his civilized force to move upon him, and by marching directly down the road, could easily reach him several hours before we could, and would probably oblige him by their numbers and annoyance to break up camp, and reach Ohio by forced marches; or if he should have heard of the capitulation by any other means, he would doubtless have lost no time in reaching a point of security for his men and valuable supplies.

Third. And then, and above all other considerations in importance, they had no ammunition to support a prolonged action;

having merely the contents of their cartridge boxes, which, on an attack of the Indian force alone, (being 600 warriors), either on the march or in position, would in all probability have been exhausted in two hours.

With this state of facts, there seemed no reasonable alternative but to send in a flag, and ascertain what disposition, if any, had been made of this part of the army, with the determination that if it was not honorable on their part, they would give battle in defense of their log houses and picket garden, and by a hard fight win an honorable surrender when victory had become impossible.

In the dusk of the evening, their flag (Captain Mansfield) returned accompanied by Colonel Elliott and Captain McKee, both heretofore mentioned.

The detachment having been included in the capitulation, marched in by the Spring

Wells road; stacked their arms opposite to, and entered the citadel—so called—being an enclosure of perhaps two acres, surrounded by sixteen foot pickets of squared cedar, within which were the officers' quarters, public stores and other buildings. It was 10 o'clock at night; repose was sought for rather than food, with the greater number, a fast of fifty-six hours, with such a tramp, and above all when attended with such extreme disappointment and mortification, had destroyed all desire for food.

The next morning, obtaining from Major Muir, the officer of the day, in immediate command, the privilege of passing from, and re-entering at pleasure, several of the volunteers of the late detachment directed their course to Smith's tavern for breakfast, after a fast of sixty-six hours.

At 12 o'clock of the 17th, the British celebrated their achievement—no one called it a victory—by firing a salute from the esplanade in front of the fort, General BROCK, with his aids, Majors MacDonnel and Glegg, appearing in full dress.

They used on this occasion one of our brass six pounders, which had been taken at the great revolutionary triumph at Saratoga, on the 16th of October, 1777, which was recorded on her in raised letters of brass. Her fire was responded to by the Queen Charlotte, their crack vessel on the upper lakes, which came sweeping up in the center of the river, and directly in front replied to each discharge, wearing ship with swan-like grace at each alternate fire.

GENERAL BROCK.

Whilst awaiting the approach in position of the vessel, General Brock, with his aids, one on each side, stood two rods from the gun, and obliquely to its left front. I had been engaged with the British Quartermaster for a supply of bateaux, in which to cross the lake to Cleveland, and being now with him on the ground, approached the gun to read the inscription, which I did with interest, when one of the Aids, noticing me, approached, and inspecting it, remarked with a smile: "*We must have an addition put to that, 'retaken at Detroit, August 16, 1812.'*" General BROCK was an officer of distinction. His personal appearance was commanding; he must have been six feet three or four inches in height; very massive and large boned, though not fleshy, and apparently of immense muscular power. His Aids were elegant young men, very near if not quite six feet in height, and in their splendid uniforms, all three presented a brilliant appearance. But how transitory and evanescent the gratification of that day and that event. In a few short weeks, less than two months, on the 13th of October, 1812, two of these noble men and gentlemanly officers, had fallen. At this distant day, I feel it due to myself and to them, to record the sentiment of regret which impressed itself upon my mind, when the announcement came that General Brock and Colonel MacDonnel, public enemies as they were, had terminated their earthly career at Queenstown.

Our much regretted brass field piece, with her glorious revolutionary record still upon her, untouched and unscathed, came again under the folds of the stars and stripes at the battle of the Thames. And the *Queen Charlotte*, the first war vessel we ever saw in full armament, which looked like "a thing of life" as she sailed up the noble stream, with her flags and streamers flaunting in the breeze, fell from her high estate of that day of gaiety and triumph, and forever ended her career of honor in that great struggle for power on the upper lakes on the 10th (tenth) day of September, 1813, when her flag descended upon a bloody wave.

I saw her afterwards dilapidated and despoiled (like some ruined mortal), performing the drudgery of a common carrier in the harbor of Buffalo.

But I am wandering from the facts and incidents of the time, and will regain my subject by bringing into view some of the agencies by which the late events were influenced; first among them was that to which I have already referred,

THE PROPOSED ARMISTICE!

Lieutenant General Sir George Prevost, Commander in Chief of the British forces in Canada—headquarters, Montreal; Major General Isaac Brock, in command of the upper province, headquarters at York (now Toronto), found themselves on the declaration of war with but a few battalions of regular troops, with which to occupy and defend all the posts from Quebec to St. Joseph.

A part of a company only was stationed at the latter place; a part of two companies of the 41st regiment at Malden; a battalion divided between Fort Erie, Fort George, and Burlington Heights, merely sufficient to take care of these posts in time of peace, and serve as centers or rallying points for the assembling of their Indian allies and the few inhabitants capable of bearing arms.

The declaration of war was unexpected! The American Government having, from the time of the Chesapeake in 1806, put up with so many injuries and indignities, it was thought in Europe that the American people could not be "kicked" into a war with England. Taken thus by surprise, and finding that the northwestern army, in great comparative force, had invaded Upper Canada early in July, these experienced Generals sought such expedients, and the creation of such temporary resources as would enable them by concentration on weak or exposed points, to divert our attention until they could receive reinforcements from home.

Finding that General Hull, instead of marching directly upon Malden with his overwhelming force, and occupying that post immediately on his invasion of that remote and defenceless portion of the upper province, as they and all other persons of military experience had expected, that he remained in his entrenched camp opposite Detroit without any apparent indications of a movement in that direction, they resolved upon a proposition of an armistice on the line of the *St. Lawrence* and the *Niagara frontier*, as an expedient most likely to afford them an advantage, by giving them an opportunity to act against General Hull, and especially to gain time, which they so much needed.

The delay of action, and cessation of hostilities, along this extensive portion of their line, which would be secured during the time of making the overture, and receiving an answer from our seat of government, especially with the then difficult and tedious means of communication, would afford them sufficient time to detach a few troops from the posts below, when, by a dash on the position of General Hull, they might succeed in frightening him into a surrender, or at least cause him to retreat from his advanced position, and evacuate the province.

To carry this stratagem into effect, Adjutant General Edward Bayne was dispatched by Lieutenant General Prevost, with a proposition for an armistice to General Dearborn, commander of the NORTHERN ARMY, at whose headquarters at Albany he arrived on the 4th of August.

The proposition was accompanied by a message delivered in the very courteous language of his accomplished Adjutant General, so diplomatic indeed that it has been adopted by the statesmen of England, when addressing themselves to the kind feelings of our ministers at her court, at times when soft words, rather than argument, could be best made use of.

"Sir GEORGE PREVOST, entertaining the
"most friendly feelings for General DEAR-
"BORN, whom he has had the honor to
"meet, * * regrets extremely that the
"two nations should have been by mere ac-
"cident precipitated into a state of war, * *
"is confident that his sovereign would meet
"an offer of peace and friendship with great
"anxiety; that all questions heretofore ex-
"isting would doubtless be settled; * * *
"that England justly engaged in a long
"and glorious war, most anxiously looked
"forward to an honorable peace with all
"the world. And above all there should be
"no war between two nations of the *same*
"*origin*, the *same laws*, and the *same*
"*religion*."

General Dearborn engaged to transmit the proposition to the President.

At that time there was no conveyance by steam power, either by water or by land; and no telegraph. The most rapid means of communication was by couriers on horseback. The object of the proposition was gained—*thirty days of time.* From Montreal to Buffalo nothing was spoken of but the "ARMISTICE!"

Flag after flag from the British side of the line announced the pleasing fact, and the assurance of the speedy settlement of all difficulties. The frontier villages of New York were tranquilized, and with the exception of these few villages, nearly the whole line of our northern frontier, from Buffalo to Vermont, was a thickly and heavily wooded wilderness.

General Brock, anticipating the success of the stratagem, proceeded to collect such force as he could prudently withdraw from his posts, and by much exertion succeeded in organizing a few militia; at the same time making arrangements for their transportation to Fort Malden, and as soon as advised, by express, of the result of the proposition, dashed ahead with his forty men of the 41st Regiment, detached from the little garrison of Fort George, and two hundred and sixty militia, striking Lake Erie at Long Point, seventy miles above Fort Erie, so as not to be seen or heard of by the Americans.

He left Long Point on the 8th, and arrived at Amherstburg, near Fort Malden, as heretofore stated, on the 12th of August. He found everything favorable.

General Hull had already broken up his camp and recrossed the river in the night of the 7th and morning of the 8th. He also received at the same time the additional and most gratifying information, obtained from intercepted dispatches, that General Hull had, at a Council of War, held prior to this date, spoken of the probability of *his having to capitulate* at no distant day.

Thus everything appeared to give assurance of success, without the risk of a battle or the loss of a man. General Hull had only to be a little *more* frightened and then summoned.

On the 13th he reconnoitered the position of his enemy, and receiving, whilst at the little village of Sandwich, a flag from General Hull, with some excuses as to the burning of a house in the afternoon after his evacuation of Canada, detained the flag until late at night, and then dispatched his Aid, Major Glegg, with the return flag to General Hull, demanding a surrender of the fort and army, as heretofore stated.

On the 14th our detachment was selected, and marched out from position near the fort.

General Brock remained quiet all this day. On the 15th he established his headquarters at Sandwich, nearly opposite "Spring Wells," making his arrangements for crossing the river. In the evening Captain Dixon's battery opened its fire upon our wagon train, stationed on the common near the fort, on its north face (the horses being in stables in the village near the river), and was replied to by our water battery of seven 24 pound long guns situated near the river at some distance above the upper angle of the esplanade, commanded by Lieutenant Daliba. No injury was done on either side.

The communication of GENERAL BROCK to GENERAL HULL, of the night of the 13th, by his Aid, Major Glegg, with a peremptory demand for the surrender of Fort Detroit, containing these words of terrifying significance to him, was subsequently redated as of this day as follows:

"Headquarters, Sandwich, Aug. 15, 1812.

"Sir, the forces at my disposal authorizes "me to require of you the IMMEDIATE SUR-"RENDER of Fort Detroit. It is far from "my inclination to join in a war of EXTER-"MINATION; but *you must be aware* that " the numerous body of INDIANS who have "attached themselves to my troops will BE

"BEYOND MY CONTROL THE MOMENT THE
"CONTEST COMMENCES," et
"ISAAC BROCK, Major General.
"His Excellency, BRIG. GEN. HULL,
"Commanding at Fort Detroit."

On the 16th, at early dawn, Dixon's battery reopened fire, which was replied to as on the previous evening, one ball only entering the fort at about 9 o'clock, as heretofore mentioned; no other damage occuring during the cannonade.

General Brock simultaneously crossed the river, and landed at "Spring Wells;" formed in column, and marched up to within ONE MILE of the fort and halted. His Indian force, organized and led by Tecumseh, under the command of Colonel Elliott and Captain McKee, landed TWO MILES below, and moved up in the edge of the woods west of the common, keeping a mile and a half distant. The strength of his force, according to his own report to Lieutenant General Prevost, was 30 Royal

Artillery, 250 41st Regiment, 50 Royal Newfoundland Regiment, 400 militia, and about 600 Indians, to which were attached three six-pounders and two three-pounders. We will now read what he says he intended to do with his little force:

"*I crossed the river with the intention of "waiting in a strong position, the effect of "our force upon the enemy's camp, in the "hope of compelling him to meet me in the "field; but receiving information upon land-"ing that Colonel McArthur, an officer of "high reputation, had left the garrison three "days before with a detachment of five hun-"dred men, and hearing soon afterwards "that his Cavalry had been seen* THAT "MORNING THREE MILES *in our rear, I "decided on an immediate attack!—by as-"sault! Brigadier General Hull, however, "prevented this movement by proposing a "cessation of hostilities,"* etc.

This is too transparent to be noticed seriously. In the first place we will look at General Hull's reply to his demand for a surrender of the fort, as of the date of the 15th, in which he uses these brave words:

"*I have no other reply to make than to inform you that I am prepared to meet any force which may be at your disposal, and any consequences which may result from any exertion of it, you may think proper to make,*" etc. And then, behold the evanescent character of all the valor that had produced this display of heroic rhetoric, when at 10 o'clock the next morning he invites his enemy to receive his surrender of the fort and army without even firing a gun!

And then as to General Brock's statement, that he first learned on his landing that morning, of the march of the detachment, when in fact the march of that detachment entered into his arrangement with General Hull on the night of the 13th; and he had been informed by his scouts every three hours, after it left the fort, of its advance into the interior; and on its march far into the interior, he well knew depended all his hopes for a consummation of the arrangements made with General Hull; and all that he says about having been informed that the "Cavalry (being the head of the column) of our detachment had been seen THAT MORNING THREE MILES IN HIS REAR," when it was, at 4 o'clock of that morning, thirty-one miles from Spring Wells, and that this fact induced him to march on the fort, and make "*an immediate assault,*" was evidently made up to help his miserable imbecile enemy, by concealing the truth of his previous arrangement with him. The whole thing, evidently gotten up in a hurry, wears a most clumsy appearance as narrated in his official report transmitted by Major Glegg, and delivered by him to Lieutenant General Prevost, at Montreal, and which, together with the flag of the 4th United States Regiment as a trophy, was forwarded by that officer to Earl Bathurst, one of the principal secretaries of State of his government, and officially published in London. To march forward with 730 men and five small guns to attack a strong fort, mounting and having under her walls twenty-six pieces of ordnance, mostly of large calibre, loaded with ball and grape, with 1940 men, posted in and around the fort, and to make an escalade without a ladder or a facine, and then with the 360 men of our detachment at his heels, pushing him in the rear, and hurrying him on, presents to the world the evidence of Quixotism or lunacy! And General Brock, most assuredly, was not the victim of either of these maladies.

To enable the future to better understand the present, I will describe some of the obstacles General Brock would have had to encounter, provided he had been in earnest as to his attempt, with his little force, to carry the fort by assault. It is a parallelogram, with strong bastions at each angle, surrounded by a moat or ditch, twelve feet wide at the surface, eight feet deep; a palisade or abbatis of hard wood stakes, ten feet high out of the ground, sharpened at the top, and firmly set in the escarp at the base of the rampart, with an inclination of about forty-five degrees.

The rampart, rising perpendicular twenty-two feet, pierced with embrasures for cannon, strong double entrance gate, with portcullis well ironed on the east front, protected by a projecting frame work of hewed logs extending over the moat, pierced for small arms, and a draw-bridge; sally ports near the southwest and northwest bastions. A parapet, banquette and terreplein around the entire of the inside, in the bastions as well as the body, on the latter of which is mounted twelve-pound and nine-pound guns, besides those of smaller calibre, and also two howitzers; each bastion having guns raking the moat and counterscarp.

Standing on the banquette near the flag staff at the southeastern angle of the body of the work, and looking southward, no house or building intervenes. All to the south for two miles, and all to the west for one to one and a half miles, is a level common.

The road from Spring Wells passes up across the public ground between the fort and the river. A few village dwellings are on the river side of this road before it reaches the public ground; and a few farm houses on the west side, the last of which is that of Mr. MAY, whose farm adjoins it, with an orchard extending back to the common, and as far as to range with the center of the southern curtain; fronting this Spring Wells' road, (and it is the only one by which the village is approached from Spring Wells,) are posted two twenty-four-pound field guns, two twelve-pound iron, and two six-pound brass guns. In front of the southern curtain, fifty feet in advance of the counterscarp, is one six-pounder; at the southwest angle is one nine-pounder and one six-pounder; in front of the western or rear curtain is one six-pounder, one four-pounder and one three-pounder; at the northwest angle one nine-pounder and one four-pounder, with arrangements to rapidly concentrate at any point at which the enemy might show himself. In May's orchard is posted the 1st Regiment of Ohio Volunteers; next to them, and extending around to the center of the west curtain, is the 2nd Regiment, and then the 3rd Regiment, which covers the northwest bastion and wagon train; whilst in the fort is the entire of the 4th United States Regiment and a part of the Artillery companies.

All these guns loaded with ball and grape; all these troops well armed, and with abundant supplies of all kinds!

The most of the village is above the public ground, and between the road and the river, and in looking from the same stand-point northward, no house or building intervenes on the line of vision, or west of it; all is a common, extending one and a half to two miles above, and one to one and a half miles westward to the edge of the original forest. Adding this to the portion south of the fort, and we see a vast open, grass covered common, on which is grazing all the cattle, and horses, and sheep of the inhabitants—scarcely a bush to be seen—*no place for Indians.* The entire of the militia of Michigan—indeed all the inhabitants, well armed and supplied, stationed by their commander, Colonel Brush, of Detroit, in positions best to protect the village.

With all these obstacles in full view, General Brock speaks of directing his Indian force, the same Indians that seven days previous had been driven from their log breast-works and forest trees by a detachment of our volunteers of about an equal number, and chased three miles to their boats, these Indians to cross an open common, and attack our camp right under the walls of the fort, whilst HE MADE HIS ASSAULT! when no one knew better than he did, that thirty minutes could not have elapsed before his whole force would have been crushed to death, or made prisoners of war!

He possibly thought, as no sensible man acquainted with the facts would believe him in earnest, he might utter a few careless words to shield his fallen foe.

AUGUST 17th.—I proceed with the incidents of the day: General Brock lost no time in returning to the Niagara frontier. Paroling the volunteers not to serve until exchanged, furnishing them with boats and vessels to pass the lake to Cleveland, sending General Hull and the regular troops to Montreal, and his militia to their homes, issuing his proclamation to the inhabitants of his conquered Territory, and leaving Colonel Proctor in command, he went on board the Queen Charlotte, and on the next day, the 18th, sailed down the lake, stopping at Fort Erie and Fort George, arriving in triumph on the 22nd at his seat of government, which he had left on the 5th; moved two hundred and fifty miles against his enemy, arriving at Malden on the 12th, demanding a surrender on the 13th, receiving it on the 16th! Achieving the conquest of a strong fort with thirty-eight pieces of ordnance, an immense amount of fixed ammunition for cannon and for small arms; a large supply of the material of war of all kinds;* an army of 2,300 effective men, AND ONE OF THE TERRITORIES OF THE UNITED STATES; all without any force of comparative strength, and all within eleven days! If he could not, with

---

* Copy of return made up by one of General Hull's Aids and the British Quartermaster in my presence, and furnished me Detroit, August 17, 1812.

Return of Ordnance, Ordnance Stores, Small Arms, Fixed Ammunition, Munitions of War, etc., surrendered

the renowned Roman, write "*Veni, vidi, vici,*" he could truly say, *I came; I demanded; I received!*

On the 30th of August, at 9 o'clock at night, Captain Pinckney, Aid-de-camp to General Dearborn, arrived at Montreal, the headquarters of Lieutenant General Sir George Prevost, with dispatches announcing the fact that "*the President of the*

---

with the Army at Fort Detroit by General Hull, and received by General Brock, 16th August, 1812.

IRON.

Twenty-four-pounders, mounted in water battery	7
Twenty-four-pounders, mounted on new field carriages	2
Twelve-pounders in and around the fort	8
Nine-pounders in and around the fort	5
Six-pounders, in and around the fort	3
Twelve-pounders, not mounted	4

BRASS.

Six-pounders at the fort	3
Four-pounders at the fort	2
Three-pounders at the fort	1
Eight-inch howitzer at the fort	1
Five and a half-inch howitzer at the fort	1
Mortar	1

Iron, 29; Brass, 9. Total, 38 pieces.

1,900 muskets and accoutrements, stacked by the effective men of the 4th United States Regiment and the Ohio

United States of America had not thought proper to authorize a continuance of the provisional measures entered into by his excellency and General Dearborn through the Adjutant General, Colonel Bayne, and that consequently the ARMISTICE *was to cease in* FOUR DAYS *from the time of the communica-*

Volunteers upon the esplanade, as they marched from their positions in and around the fort.
700 do., do., brought in by the militia of Michigan, and stacked upon the esplanade.
450 do., do., brought in by the detachment and the corps of teamsters, and stacked in front of the citadel; also a large supply in the arsenal.
480 rounds of fixed ammunition for twenty-four pounders.
600 rounds of fixed ammunition for six-pounders.
840 rounds of fixed ammunition for twelve-pounders and other pieces.
200 cartridges of grape shot for six-pounders.
200 tons of cannon balls of different sizes.
480 shells prepared and charged for mortar and howitzers.
60 barrels of gunpowder.
75,000 musket cartridges made up.
25 rounds of cartridges with each man is 75,300.
150 tons of lead.
25 day's provisions on hand at the fort, beside the supplies at the river Raisin.

These words added by W. S. H.: "With an abundance of subsistence in the vicinity, beside the great number of cattle, sheep and horses feeding on the common."

tion reaching Montreal and the posts of Kingston and Fort George." Thus terminated the proposed armistice.

I now proceed to give a sketch of one who has already exerted great influence as an auxiliary in the events narrated, and who, from this time forward, fills a conspicuous and important station, and wields a controlling power in the future progress of the war in the northwest—the renowned Indian chief, the greatest of his race,

TECUMSEH.

I am aware that prejudice has at all times so influenced the mind of many persons, that they would not admit the existence of the attribute of greatness in any of the Indian race; at the same time they readily admitted that this extraordinary man exerted an immense influence over all the Indian tribes, and possessed distinguished abilities as a warrior and orator. It is, however, very clear, from the character and power of his mind, evidenced by his unlimited control over all others of his race for so long a time. The large and extended views and combinations requisite to draw into his league all the tribes from the Rocky Mountains to New York, and from Lake Superior to Florida; the unlimited devotion to his service and to himself, together with his great power as an orator, by which he swayed them and controlled them; all these furnished conclusive evidence of greatness, and of his being entitled to that high appellation.

Tecumseh was nothing less than a great man, not of the first-class, as that is very limited; his birth formed an epoch in his tribal annals, from the circumstance of which he was looked upon as a prodigy from his first existence. *He was one and the youngest of three brothers at the same birth.* This event, so extraordinary among the Indian tribes, with whom even a double birth is quite uncommon, struck the mind of his people as supernatural, and marked him and his brothers with the prestige of future greatness — that the Great Spirit would direct them to the achievement of something great.

They were born in a cabin or hut, constructed of round saplings chinked with sticks and clay, near the mouth of Stillwater, on the upper point of its junction, with the Great Miami, then a pleasant plateau of land, with a field of corn not subject to overflow.

These facts were communicated to me a short time after the council at Springfield in 1806, (in the presence of Colonel Robert Patterson, one of the original proprietors of Cincinnati,) by General Simon Kenton, who was more familiar with the Indian chiefs and Indian tribes of the northwest, at the period of their greatest power, both in war and in peace, than any other man. He stated that he well knew all the brothers; had been in the cabin, so situated, where they and the family lived, and that other Indians, whom he knew to be perfectly reliable, and who were intimately acquainted with the family of Tecumseh, had fully confirmed the above statement, as to the triple birth, and the location of their parents' residence at the time of their birth.

I am more particular in this account, as both the circumstances and place of their birth, have been variously stated by others, and particularly in what appear as the recollections of Colonel Dale, as written out by the Hon. Mr. Claiborne. It is very clear that Colonel Dale's recollections on this point were erroneous. His information must have referred to a remote ancestor of Tecumseh, as having married a Cherokee, perhaps his grandfather or great grandfather, instead of his father. If such a marriage ever took place, it must have been before the migration, which was as early as 1730. His father and mother undoubtedly were both of the Shawanee nation; and it is utterly out of the question that TECUMSEH could have been born on the Tallapoosa.

The Shawanees previous to their migration from North and South Carolina and Georgia, (as they had villages in all these states), were generally on good terms with both the Cherokees and Creeks; and when they did migrate, crossed the Cumberland Mountains, through the Cumberland Gap, and passed on through the great hunting ground of all the western tribes, (now the State of Kentucky), striking the waters of the Sandy River, descending along its course to the Ohio, which they crossed at the mouth of the Scioto; at which time they were full two thousand warriors strong. They ascended that stream, established their villages "OLD TOWN," on Paint Creek; at the *Pickaway Plains*, "OLD CHILLICOTHE," above the present site of Xenia, Greene county, (on the *ruins* of which Harmar long afterwards encamped, when his first detachment sent out to find them was so terribly worsted,)* and on the Great Miami, between where Dayton now stands, and Piqua, in Miami county. As I knew them, they were truly noble specimens of their race, universally of fine athletic forms, and light complexions,

---

* At the commencement of the Anglo-Indian war of 1791, which I have spoken of in another place, so little was known of the north-western territory, its geography, the position and course of *its rivers*, that in respect even to that portion of it now included within the State of Ohio, many errors of description were made and published.

The confluence of the Muskingum, the Scioto, the Miamis of the south with the Ohio, were well known, but their branches or affluents were involved in obscurity. To this cause we may very reasonably attribute the errors of HARMAR, made in his reports to the Secretary of War, describing the *places* where his conflicts with the Indians took place during his ill-fated campaign.

Harmar was from the east of the Alleghanies, an officer of the regular army, with no apparent capacity to conduct a campaign against such an enemy.

He marched with three hundred and twenty regulars from Ft. Washington, (a stockade enclosure with block-houses; its site now between Broadway and Ludlow streets, divided by Third street in the City of Cincinnati,) on the 30th of September, 1791, with orders to destroy the Shawanee Indian villages, on the Scioto, and then unite with the troops from

none more so, and none appeared their equal, unless it was their tribal relatives, the Ottoways, who adjoined them. The warriors of these tribes were the finest looking Indians I ever saw, and were truly noble specimens of the human family.

None, as they *then were*, are now to be seen upon the earth! They have all passed

---

Kentucky, then on the Wabash, and advance to the Miami of Lake Erie, destroying all Indian villages on the upper and head waters of the Great Miami, the St. Mary's, and wherever found by the combined forces.

He advanced northward about twenty-five miles, to a position on the Great Miami, at which Fort Hamilton was established in the following year, by General St. Clair, and there united with the Volunteer Militia troops from Kentucky and Pennsylvania, who had as the main part of his army already moved in advance, those from Kentucky being under the command of General Hardin; his entire combined force amounting to fourteen hundred and fifty-three men. After considerable time employed in making his arrangements, and bringing on supplies, he moved northeastwardly upon the chief town of the Shawanees, " CHILLICOTHE," situated about six miles north of the present site of Xenia, Greene county, at which for many years the grand councils of the tribes of the north-west had been held, when consulting on their general interest, and especially in their long continued struggle to prevent the occupancy of their great hunting ground by the white race.

This celebrated town was on an eminence fronting and

away! None but the vilest dregs of any of the Indian tribes of the old northwestern territory now remain.

Those who understand the immense influence exercised over the minds of these people, by what they believe to be supernatural events, special workings of the Great Spirit, will not be surprised at the

---

overlooking the rich meadows of the Little Miami. Its remains I examined as early as 1806, at which time numerous articles of Indian construction and use, stone battle axes, arrow heads, and various other things were scattered over the ground.

On Harmar's approach he found the smoking ruins of a burned and abandoned village; not an Indian to be seen. They had sacrificed their "MOSCOW," and retired *ten miles* in the direction of the confluence of Mad River and the Great Miami; took up an advantageous position, and *awaited* Harmar's movements, who played into their hands by sending a small detachment under General Hardin of but two hundred and ten men to attack them. This little detachment they cut to pieces. Harmar then sent his forces to the Scioto, who destroyed without resistance their towns and their crops on the borders of that stream; when, as he alleged, having lost several of his horses, he abandoned the idea of joining the Kentucky forces on the Wabash, and broke up camp in order to return to Fort Washington; but as he had not at this time become possessed of his brilliant ideas in regard to "VICTORIES," "*he felt desirous,*" as he said, "*of wiping off in another*" action the disgrace which his

fact that when General Kenton was at the residence of this family, as heretofore mentioned, he found undiminished faith in anticipated achievements and benefits destined to be wrought and triumphantly secured to their tribe and race, by one or more of these remarkable brothers.

In partial fulfillment of this anticipated

---

arms had sustained." He halted about *eight miles* from his camp, (the ruins of "Chillicothe,") "*late at night,*" and again detached General Hardin with but "*three hundred and sixty men to find the enemy, and bring him to action.*" EARLY THE NEXT MORNING that intrepid and brave officer reached the confluence of Mad River and the Great Miami, where he found the Indians in great force; who with skillful manoeuvers brought him within their lines when his little detachment was, as in the case of the first, overwhelmed and nearly all destroyed. The skeleton of Hardin's little force regained head-quarters.

Now it was that Harmar in making his official report to the Secretary of War, conceived the grand idea of claiming as signal victories his two engagements with the enemy, alleging that inasmuch as the United States with their vast population would not feel the loss of *one hundred* men as much as the Indians with their inferior number would feel the loss of *one* man, therefore he had obtained "*two signal victories over them.*"

Chief Justice Marshall, however, in recording these events could not see it in that light; and history with unrelenting destiny, one of the brothers was soon afterwards proclaimed and publicly acknowledged as the "PROPHET OF THE GREAT SPIRIT," whilst another of them, TECUMSEH, who at the council held at Springfield, in 1806, to which I have heretofore referred, fully established his reputation as the great orator of his race, and rose to the distinguished station of leader and chief warrior of all the tribes of the northwest. As this

---

obstinacy, persists in calling such a complete cutting up and slaughter a defeat instead of a victory.

Yet with all his knowledge on every other subject, so great was the obscurity in respect to the geography of our old north-western territory at that time, that the learned and astute Chief Justice inadvertently copied HARMAR when he describes this last action as having taken place at the junction of the "ST. JOSEPH AND ST. MARY," when in fact Harmar was not within one hundred miles of that important position.

He returned to Fort Washington, and the few who formed the then *little village* of CINCINNATI, condemned him for having fought his enemy with small detachments, instead of his whole army.

This last action, just above the junction of Mad River with the Great Miami, was the time and the field in which, as I have stated in another place, TECUMSEH, then a mere lad of 16 years of age, made his advent as a youthful warrior.

council was the time and the occasion, when his power and abilities as an orator were first brought to the knowledge of the public, and became fully acknowledged by our agents and citizens, as well as the Indian chiefs, who attended it, I will describe it.

A white man had been shot and killed in the woods not far from the present site of Troy, in Miami county; it was charged upon a Pottawatamie. The United States Indian agents, General Kenton and Colonel Patterson, demanded that he should be given up to be tried and punished according to our laws in conformity to treaty stipulations. The demand was evaded. The Indians were called in to hold a council on the matter at Springfield, Clarke county, then a new settlement of a dozen families. Three hundred Indians, from various tribes assembled; all armed to the teeth. They were of course required to leave their arms, except their side arms, the tomahawk, (which was at that time made with the head so formed as to be a bowl of a pipe, with a hole in the handle through which to draw the smoke,) at their encampment on the creek, nearly a mile distant.

The council was opened as usual, by passing round the diplomatic pipe, the Indian emblem of peace, and token of amity and good will. The oldest chief present, Tarfee (or the Crane), principal chief of the Wyandots, one of the signers of the treaty of Greenville, 1795, commenced the ceremony; none but chiefs and chief warriors were present, and they were all members of the council. They were arranged in a semi-circle, in front of the agent's stand. The ceremonies being concluded, the agent made a statement of the object of the council, the fact of the murder, the demand for the murderer, and the evident reluctance on the part of the Indians to comply with their treaty stipulations, and preserve a good state of feeling and conduct on their part towards us. The old chief of the Wyandots, and the chief of the Ottoways replied in a conciliatory style, with the usual expressions of good faith, and the desire to live on good terms with their white brethren, etc. All was apparently going on satisfactorily, when Tecumseh arose and commenced his address. He continued his oration for three hours; commencing with the first aggressions of the white men, and bringing down his traditional history from the first settlement at Jamestown and Plymouth to his own time. The effect of his bitter, burning words of eloquence was so great on his companions, that the whole three hundred warriors could hardly refrain from springing from their seats. Their eyes flashed, and even the most aged; many of whom were smoking, evinced the greatest excitement. The orator appeared in all the power of a fiery, and impassioned speaker and actor. Each moment it seemed as though, under the influence of his overpowering eloquence, they would all abruptly leave the council and defiantly return to their homes.

On the conclusion of his address Tecumseh stood for a moment, turned his back upon the agent's stand, and walking to the extremity of the circle opposite, took his seat among the young braves, glancing with lofty pride upon the agents. The interpreter then proceeded to give his version of the speech, but confessed afterwards that there were portions of it so grand, lofty, and powerful, that he could not pretend to reproduce them, and that there were other portions in which he had been describing the wrongs of the Indian race, inflicted by the white man, that were so defiant, so wrathful, so denunciatory, and so full of indignant abuse, that he dare not translate them, fearing that General Kenton would not put up with it, and that it might cause the breaking up of the council, and leave unsettled the important matter for which it had been called. On further consultation a reconciliation of the so nearly hostile parties took place. It being proved that the murder was the act of an individual as yet unknown, and not properly chargeable on any of the Indian tribes.

It was not that there was any diminution in the power which Tecumseh exercised over the minds of all the tribes, nor any diminution of their confidence in his genius and destiny, that caused him to be left in July, 1812, with but sixty warriors, nor was it that the hostile feeling on his part or on that of his Indian allies had in any measure lessened since the conflict at Tippecanoe, on the 7th of November previous; nor had the incessant efforts of the British official agents to keep alive, and if possible increase that hostility, in any way been diminished or neglected. On the contrary, as the probabilities of war between the two countries, increased, and became more apparent, they redoubled their active exertions to excite the Indians to the greatest degree of ferocity against us.

They enlarged and greatly added to the variety and value of their usual presents, furnished them abundantly with arms and ammunition from Malden, and took every means calculated to cement their bonds of friendship with them.

The only cause of the diminution of the indian force under Tecumseh, at this time, was the display of power made by the marching columns of the northwestern army, in full view, over the wide prairies and open barrens between the rapids of the Maumee and the river Raisin.

They appeared to be impressed with the belief that any effort on their part with their force, then in arms, whilst their British friends were so feeble in number and power, as they then were at Malden, would be unavailing of success against so great an army as ours. Therefore, three hundred and fifty warriors, who had participated in the battle of Tippecanoe, and up to this time were still held in council at Brownstown, between the Huron and Detroit, desirous of war, in their cause, anxious to keep on the best of terms with their powerful allies, from whom they received all their supplies, and, above all, unwilling to separate, even for a season, from their great leader. Yet seeing this great disparity of force, with no reasonable prospect of success, they all, with the exception of about one hundred of his most devoted followers, reluctantly abandoned for the time their then hopeless cause, and returned to their tribes, and in the event of the capture of Malden, which no one doubted for a moment, they would not have again appeared in hostility against us. There would have been no Indian war; no massacre at Fort Dearborn, (Chicago), or at the river Raisin; none of that vast waste of valuable life, independent of the slain resulting from exposure, fatigue, privation and suffering in the swamps of the northwestern wilderness, during the next ensuing two years.

Those who have been familiar with the Indians of the northwest, when they *were* Indians, and took sufficient interest in them as a race to study with care their customs, laws and usages, are aware that when attending councils with other nations or tribes, or with our agents, they are always *acting a part*, a kind of diplomatic drama, and that their "*war dance*" is really a PANTOMIME, exhibiting their art of war. The declaration, the march upon their enemy, the near approach indicated by their crouching attitude, stealthy step and anxious, piercing look—the sight of their enemy; their yell and frantic dash upon him; their struggle in a hand to hand contest; the blows of the war club, and wielding of the tomahawk; the crushing and destruction of their foe; the flashing of the inevitable scalping knife, triumphantly closing the scene with the evidence of victory; the bloody scalp held high in air, and greeted with a horrid yell! All the ancient nations had their war cry; the Greek, the Roman, the Carthagenian, all had their inspiring shout of onset at the commencement of a battle. Who has not heard of the *slogan* of the Scottish Highlander? Yet I doubt not the "*war whoop*" and "*yell*" of our Indians of the old northwestern Territory, was more terrific than any of them.

It has been remarked that nearly all the races of which the human family is composed, possess some distinguishing characteristic feature, indicative of their ferocity, brutality, or of their refinement or benevolence. The descendant of Ishmael, the *Arab of the desert*, is said to carry the evidence of his treachery and cruelty, which have defied the influence of civilization for thirty centuries, in the form and expression of his mouth; whilst our old northwestern Indians, almost without exception, as I observed them with interest, with the beautiful mouth and teeth of the Greek in his highest civilization, presented to the observer the evidence of his ferocity and savageism, as well as his determined bravery, in his fiery eye! He is proud, candid, confiding in time of peace, never forgetting a kindness, or forgiving an injury; not treacherous, except as a part of his war tactics, and brave in the fullest sense of the term.

Such were the Indians of the old Shawanee, Ottoway, Miami and Delaware tribes, with whom I was most familiar, both in times of war and peace, in councils, in camps, on fields of conflict, and in peaceful intercourse, in the years 1804 to 1816.

The Wyandotts, Chippeways, Winnebagoes, Pottawattomies and Kickapoos, occupying the northwestern Territory, at the same time, always appeared to me as inferior branches of the race. The superior and the inferior, alike however, have passed away, and given place to a race charged with a higher destiny, leaving behind them none but the shattered and wronged remnants of a mighty people, who, in fulfilling the inscrutable decrees of Providence in regard to them, yet linger upon the earth, many of them the miserable victims to the degrading vices of a boastful but treacherous and cruel civilization.

The Indians occupying the geographical limits of the United States, and British possessions north of us, possess two exalted qualities of mind, lofty principles of action, noble traits of individuality, unchangeable, inherent, which, if accompanied by civilization, would have ranked them above all other races of men, and even without this, and in their present degraded, fallen condition, claim for them the sympathy, if they can not receive the respect, of all honorable and good men.

They never worshiped idols.

They never were slaves.

They acknowledged one great, creating, overruling GOD, to whom they applied the perfectly correct term, the "GREAT SPIRIT," whose power they beheld in the storm, the lightning, the thunder and the whirlwind; whose goodness and benign influence they saw and felt in the genial breeze, the early flower, the growing grass of the spring, the fowl of the air, the fish of every water, the multitude of animals given for their use, and feeding on every plain, and every hill, and in every solitude; and when they laid down at night, they beheld His starry canopy above them brilliant and glorious; whilst all around them was their dominion and their home. They abhor as a crime, and lament as a loss, the wanton, reckless destruction of those God-given means of subsistence, so barbarously and cruelly indulged in by our portion of the white race.

Always free! Every other race, every other people of the earth, are and have been slaves!

The BLACK race, always slaves abroad,

and worse slaves to their brutal tyrants at home!

The YELLOW race, never free, since their earliest tribal existence

The WHITE race, the enslavers of all others, as well as themselves, ALWAYS SLAVES in some form, they surrender their sovereign power of self-government, and yield their liberty and manhood to a SAUL, or to a monied Aristocracy, a corrupt central power with a great public debt, either of which enslaves them; whilst the INDIAN walks forth upon the earth free as the air he breathes, knowing no superior, but the ever glorious Almighty GOD who made him, with a sublime pride, always ready to surrender his life, but never his liberty! Never basely DISHONORING HIMSELF by becoming the slave of his equal in creation, nor OFFENDING, in the highest degree, the EVER GLORIOUS BLESSED SPIRIT, by vilely *deserting* and abandoning the *post* of *honor*, the highest front rank of his earthly creation *assigned him,* and by his own infamy becoming the mere co-worker and co-equal of the brute.

So has it always been with the black race!

So has it always been with the yellow race!

So has it always been with the white race; and so has it always been with our old indian race!

I place this upon record, as there can *never* be another " Phillip," or " Pontiac," or " Tecumseh !"

The renowned " Prophet " lost his prestige and influence by precipitating his unsuccessful attack upon our army at Tippecanoe, on the 7th November, whilst Tecumseh was absent on his mission to the Chickasaws, Cherokees, Seminoles, old allies of his tribe, arranging his plans, and bringing into his confederation or league all the tribes, to regain if possible their old boundaries, and at all events to resist the further encroachments of the white race,* hav-

* TECUMSEH sought to establish it as the great national law of all the tribes, that no one tribe or nation should have the power to sell any part of their land, without the consent of all the tribes or nations; and in his endeavors to establish this great principle, he visited many times, devoting all his energies and great talents with unceasing effort, every nation and tribe this side the Rocky Mountains, and from Lake Superior to the ocean, and at the same time combining all the Indian nations in a grand confederacy, to support this general law, by a war of resistance to the people of the United States in their encroachments upon them. This great subject employed every day of his time and every power of his mind, from the year 1804 to 1813, when himself and his cause perished forever.

At an official conference with General Harrison, then Governor of the Indiana Territory, at Vincennes, in 1810, in answer to a question on the subject by the General, he asserted his policy openly and fully, that he was forming a grand confederacy of all the nations and tribes of Indians upon the continent, for the purpose of putting a stop to the encroachments of the white people; and in his argument in defense of his course, said, that "the policy which the United States pursued of purchasing in unceasing detail their lands from the separate Indian tribes, he viewed as a *mighty water*, ready to overflow his people, and that the confederacy which he was forming among the tribes to *prevent* any individual tribe from selling without the consent of the others, was the DAM he was erecting to resist this *mighty water.*" He added in conclusion: " *Your great Father may sit over the mountains and drink his wine; but if he continues this policy you and I will have to fight it out!*

And so it was. These two highly distinguished men did "fight it out." This "prophetic" declaration was verified.

ing given positive orders before leaving his camps on the Vermillion and at Tippecanoe, two months previous to the battle, that no attack upon the white man should be attempted, or in any way made in his absence. He was, therefore, greatly surprised and exceedingly indignant, when on his return, and reaching the upper Chickasaws, in western Tennessee, he heard that his brother had brought on and fought a premature and unsuccessful action; thereby interfering with his views, deranging his proposed plans, and above all, disobeying his orders as the universally acknowledged war chief of all.

From this time the "PROPHET" ceased to have influence, fell into obscurity, and was soon forgotten, or not thought of amidst the rapid changes and absorbing interests of the ever occurring vicissitudes of a general war.

TECUMSEH.

The personal appearance of this remarkable man was uncommonly fine. His height was about five feet nine inches, judging him by my own height when standing close to him, and corroborated by the late Colonel John Johnston, for many years Indian Agent at Piqua. His face oval rather than angular; his nose handsome and straight; his mouth beautifully formed, like that of Napoleon I, as represented in his portraits; his eyes clear, transparent hazel, with a mild, pleasant expression when in repose, or in conversation; but when excited in his orations, or by the enthusiasm of conflict, or when in anger, they appeared like balls of fire; his teeth beautifully white, and his complexion more of a light brown or tan than red; his whole tribe as well as their kindred, the Ottoways, had light complexions; his arms and hands were finely formed; his limbs straight; he always stood very erect, and walked with a brisk, elastic, vigorous step; invariably dressed in Indian tanned buckskin; a perfectly well fitting hunting frock, descending to the knee, was over his under clothes of the same material; the usual cape and finish of leather fringe about the neck; cape, edges of the front opening, and bottom of the frock; a belt of the same material, in which were his side arms (an elegant silver-mounted tomahawk, and a knife in a strong leather case), short pantaloons, connected with neatly fitting leggins and moccasins, with a mantle of the same material thrown over his left shoulder, used as a blanket in camp, and as a protection in storms. Such was his dress when I last saw him, on the 17th of August, 1812, on the streets of Detroit; mutually exchanging tokens of recognition as former acquaintance, in years of peace, and passing on, he, to see that his Indians had all crossed to Malden, as commanded, and to counsel with his white allies in regard to the next move.

ment of the now really commenced war of 1812. He was then in the prime of life, and presented in his appearance and noble bearing one of the finest looking men I have ever seen.

After the massacre at Fort Dearborn, in which he had no participation, being far distant, and the investment of Fort Wayne, we next see this chieftain in command of three thousand three hundred organized warriors,* surrounding Fort Meigs at the Maumee rapids, with his sword by his side, recognized as a BRIGADIER GENERAL in the

---

* Eight hundred of the most valiant of whom were well mounted; the principal officers armed with carbine rifles, pistols, tomahawk and knife, at whose head he, with his ever attending suite of young braves, the sons of principal warriors, rode up the line of the Maumee, challenging General Harrison to come out of Fort Meigs, and give him battle. His challenge was in these words:

"GENERAL HARRISON,"

"*I have with me eight hundred braves. You have an equal number in your hiding place. Come out with them and give me battle: You talked like a brave when we met at Vincennes, and I respected you; but now you hide behind logs and in the earth, like a ground hog. Give me answer.*"

"TECUMSEH."

British service, and, after General Brock, he was the only general officer of talent or honorable conduct in the English army of the northwest.*

Colonel Proctor, about this time promoted to the rank of brigadier general, and soon afterwards to that of major general, was one of the meanest looking men I ever saw. He had an expression of countenance

---

* I have noticed that some writers have been in doubt whether TECUMSEH understood or could speak our language. He did understand, and could speak nearly all the words in common use sufficiently so to hold conversation on ordinary topics; but he never spoke any but his own language at any council, or when in presence of any officer or agent of any government; nor would he attempt to speak in any but his own language when in company with any one, except with those toward whom he felt very friendly, or had private intercourse, and who did not understand his own language.

He always avoided speaking to any official agent of the British, or our government, except through his interpreter. His reasons were, that he especially desired not to be misunderstood; he would not have his ideas misapprehended if he could prevent it; and he was aware that in any discussion in language not perfectly comprehended, verbal and often very important mistakes would occur. His ideas of the honor of his people and race, precluded any official intercouse in any but the Shawanee language.

in which that of the murderer and cowardly assassin predominated; nor did he belie his appearance. His infamous massacre, or permitting the massacre of wounded prisoners at Winchester's defeat, at the river Raisin, placed him beyond the pale of civilized warfare, and subjected him, according to the universal verdict of public opinion, to have been shot down as an outlaw, whenever or wherever afterwards met by any western man, especially by any Kentuckian.

That there should be vile, cowardly, and of course, cruel Indians to act as the willing instruments of such atrocity, is not to be considered singular, as no army has ever moved, whether American or Indian, but has been, and now is, infested with these most detestable followers. This, however, is always an *exception*, and never chargeable to the *valiant, honorable, brave,* and of course *humane* warrior of whatever race.

It was well for us that on our second entrance into Canada, in 1813, the counsels of Tecumseh did not prevail. At a council of war, held at Malden, previous to the approach of our army under General Harrison, he urged upon General Proctor the necessity of meeting the invading forces as they landed below Amherstburg, and if there overpowered by superior numbers, to retire upon their line of retreat, and take up the strong position, protected by an extensive forest and deep water, at the crossing of the Canard river. If driven from this position, to take another near the river Thames, retiring with all their supplies protected, and disputing every advance, until our army should be drawn far into the interior, beyond the Moravian towns, when, if necessary, all the forces of the upper province, such as could be brought from Burlington Heights, or other posts, could join them, and by continued harassing and vigorous struggles they would exhaust and overwhelm us, or at least oblige us to retreat and leave the province.

These views, however correct and sound, met with no response from General Proctor. He, on the contrary, ordered a rapid flight! Tecumseh rose abruptly to his feet, dashed his sword violently upon the table, and in a great rage denounced Proctor as a coward, "A MISERABLE OLD SQUAW," turned upon his heel and left the room. *

Proctor lost no time in endeavoring to appease the wrath of his great Indian ally, by promising him that he would fight the invaders at the crossing of the Canard

---

* General Harrison appreciated the soundness of these views as well as the talent and judgment of Tecumseh, if Proctor did not. In his communication to the Governor of Ohio, dated at Detroit, Oct. 11, 1813, six days after the battle of the THAMES, he says:

"*Nothing but infatuation could have governed General Proctor's conduct. The day that I landed below Malden, he had at his disposal upwards of three thousand Indians.* The INDIANS were EXTREMELY DESIROUS OF FIGHTING US AT MALDEN. I enclose you TECUMSEH's communication or speech to PROCTOR. IT IS AT ONCE THE EVIDENCE OF THE TALENTS OF THE FORMER, AND THE GREAT DEFECT OF THEM IN THE LATTER," etc.

river and at the mouth of the Thames; that he would meet him on his landing, but for the fact that the enemy had all the ships and great guns upon them, with which he could kill them without their being able to reach him with their guns; that he did not think it reasonable or proper to make a stand until he reached the woods of the Canard. When he arrived at the crossing of this stream, instead of fulfilling his promise, he again excused himself to Tecumseh, by stating that the Americans were bringing their ships up the Detroit river, and could fire in upon their flank with their "DOUBLE BALLS," as Tecumseh called the shells, (of which he had a very high opinion, from witnessing their effect at the siege of Fort Meigs), whilst they were engaged in battle with them in front. Therefore he proposed to continue his march to the vicinity of the mouth of the Thames, and there select his ground and fight them, out of reach of their ships.

On arriving at the place designated, he plead another excuse, that, although the Americans could not bring up their ships, into the Thames, they could place their cannon in boats, and thus use them in the battle; and, therefore, it would be best for him to march still further up the river, and into the interior so far that the water would be too shoal for the passage of their boats.

Tecumseh saw that Proctor did not intend to fight; that instead of offering the Americans battle, his sole object was to escape from them; that his previous promises were false and deceptive; and knowing that all hope of success in his cause [1.]—all prospect of achieving an advantage in his war against us, depended on the defeat of the American army, or obliging it to retire, after being harassed and fought in the wilds of Canada, he assumed the superiority that he possessed over him; again denounced him for his cowardice, as well as his evident treachery, declaring his intention from thenceforth, to act as the chief commander, to which his own force entitled him, prohibited Proctor's advance, proclaiming that HE would march in advance, select his battle ground, and if Proctor would not fight the enemy, he would have him SCALPED!

Tecumseh moved in advance, selected his ground, and it was well selected, fixed upon his plan of battle, put his forces in line, reviewed every rod of the field, and spoke to and gave orders to each of his chiefs; obliged General Proctor to occupy the position assigned him—and it was the proper one.

The battle of the " Thames" was fought! And whilst, from the moment that Colonel Johnson's regiment of mounted infantry prepared to charge on the British front, the commander of the British forces was seen fleeing for his life, the Indian chieftain made his gallant stand upon his own and last selected battle ground; and history has to record the fact, that when at last

General PROCTOR was forced to give battle on the field selected by TECUMSEH, he vilely fled, and left the unfought field, his forces and his allies; whilst the heroic warrior, with the bravery ever shown by his nation and his race, breasted the storm of a crushing battle charge. And having fulfilled his duties as a great and humane warrior, [2] and his destiny as chief commander in his great cause, which was no other than the cause of his race and people; having achieved all that Providence permitted to be achieved in their behalf, closed in honor his earthly career [3].

In closing this chapter, I will again recur to the surrender of Fort Detroit and the northwestern army, by General Hull.

There was no man of intelligence in the army who did not believe, at the time, that the surrender had been pre-arranged between General Hull and General Brock, who was well known to be an officer of experience, and of high reputation, and when HE MARCHED up his little force, as heretofore described, halted the head of his column in open view, and right in front of our batteries, beside the entire armament of the fort bearing on him, this general belief became irresistable. That this belief and these conclusions were entirely correct, the full, complete and perfect evidence afterwards obtained, as herein stated, has fully proven and confirmed beyond any doubt.

The only uncertainty upon the mind of any one was, whether the surrender was negotiated from first to last by General Hull, under the direct influence of treason, or whether it was from cowardice. The evidence of cowardice was certainly exhibited by him. The first verdict of the entire army was, "TREASON," and this verdict was evidently a true verdict; but whether it was the treason of the commanding general, or the treason of others operating on his extreme timidity, was the only question, and remains in history the only question.

General Hull's official report of his surrender, dated at Fort George, Canada, August 26, 1812, is filled with misstatements, evidently intended to extenuate his conduct and his acts. Some of his statements and reasons are really childish. He appears to be struggling under the pressure of conscious guilt to stem and avert the influence of an indignant public opinion, which, in unison with the opinion of the army, had passed upon him.

He says, in reference to the difficulty of obtaining supplies for the army from Ohio, that "*on this extensive road, two hundred miles through a wilderness, it depended for transportation of provisions, military stores, medicine, clothing, and every other supply,* on PACK HORSES;" instead of which the army had marched along that road, but six weeks previous, with an ample wagon train,* conveying *all the tents, baggage, stores, ammunition and equipage* of the army, drawn by HORSES and OXEN; *not a single "*PACK HORSE*" was used on the march.*

He further asserts, that on the 15th of August, "*the whole effective force at his disposal at Detroit did not exceed* 800 *men.*" This is so glaringly false, that it is really a matter of wonder that he should have asserted it, especially as he knew that the daily reports of the condition of the army were regularly made up, and reported by

---

* The late Presley Kemper, of Walnut Hills, a well known and respected citizen, and for some years one of the commissioners of Hamilton County, was wagon master of this train. He, with his train, had crossed over into Canada on the same day that the army crossed over, occupied a position in the entrenched camp, and his corps of teamsters had been supplied with fifty-two muskets, cartridge boxes, and ammunition. His train of *fifty-one large four horse Pennsylvania wagons, recrossed the river on the night of the 7th and morning of the 8th of August,* to the position assigned to them *on the common,* in a line northward from the northwest bastion of the fort, and close to it, and remained there in *full view of General Hull's headquarters, until after the surrender.*

the brigade major, acting as adjutant general, afterwards, and up to the day of his death, quartermaster general of the United States army, the late General Thomas S. Jesup. And these reports showed, what every officer knew to be true, that there were nineteen hundred effective men at the fort on the evening of the 15th and morning of the 16th. There were, also, in the vicinity, our detachment of three hundred and sixty effective men, Colonel Brush's command at the river Raisin, and the entire militia of Michigan.

General Brock, in his report to Lieutenant General Prevost, officially transmitted to London, and there officially published, sets down the number of our troops surrendered to him, including Brush's command, and not including the militia of Michigan, at twenty-five hundred men. In this he was correct, as all except Brush's force were set down by name, and recorded when parolled, and sent home or taken to Montreal.

Again, in speaking of the troops, "*having performed a laborious march; having been engaged in a number of battles and skirmishes, in which many had fallen, and more had received wounds;* in addition to which a large number being sick, *and unprovided with medicine, and the comforts necessary to their situation.*"

So far from this being the case, the army had a comparatively easy march through the woods, at the most pleasant season of the year, from the last of May to the first of July, not too hot or too cold, with abundant supplies of all kinds, having first-rate new tents; no forced marches, but frequent halts, only sufficient exercise to keep the army in good health; and then it had been *for a month at the end of its march*, with but few reconnoisances in force, or skirmishes, or battles.

Instead of being sickly, it was remarkably healthy, and in fine condition in every respect. Very few were wounded or on the sick list; and as to the "*sick being unprovided with medicine, and the comforts necessary to their situation,*" the assertion was sheer nonsense, independent of being entirely destitute of truth.

The annunciation of his surrender shocked the whole country, and fell with stunning force upon the mind of every man west of the mountains.

It appeared incredible that a numerous and well appointed army, with a strong fortress, could be surrendered to the enemy with his feeble force, without a battle or disaster of any kind. But so it was; and by this act a great and bloody Indian war was brought upon us.

The great gate of the northwest was thrown wide open; free access to our unprotected frontier settlements was given, the dark hordes of the wilderness rushed UPON them; they were all destroyed. The wild WAR WHOOP not only "*awakened the sleep of the cradle,*" whilst the "*flames of our dwellings illumined the path of the savage;*' but its fearful echoes broke upon the silence of night, along all our borders, all our wilderness frontier, with terrific force, and warned the stoutest hearts to a present and bloody conflict.

HIS CAUSE.

I have already noticed the "CAUSE," the great object for which Tecumseh labored, and devoted all his time and all his power, from the time of his arriving at manhood, to the day when he laid down his life for it. His celebrated predecessor, "PONTIAC," urged on and encouraged by the French traders and inhabitants of Canada, hoped to overwhelm the English colonists, and force them to abandon all the country, except that contained within a narrow boundary along the sea shore. And when he had driven in the inhabitants of Pennsylvania almost to the Susquehannah, leaving but a few weak posts in the possession of the white man, he felt assured of success. And it was not until "BOUQUET," one of the ablest and most skillful commanders that ever marched an army against our northwestern Indians, had beaten them at "BUSHY RUN," and relieved Fort Pitt, and the gallant Gladwin had most nobly maintained a protracted and vigorously conducted siege of Fort Detroit, in which "PONTIAC," in person, displayed his greatest force, and exerted all his subtle strategy and skill, that finally paralyzed his efforts, and caused him, most reluctantly, to yield to the conviction that without the aid of ordnance, the skill to manage it, and the munitions of war possessed by the white man, it would be unavailing of success for him to attempt the reduction of forts and strongly fortified posts. With these impressions, which forced themselves upon his judgment, he saw that his great struggle would be hopeless unless aided by some one of the nations of the white race; therefore he slowly yielded the field, and closed, for the time being, his efforts in his great CAUSE.

From the termination of this great war of PONTIAC, 1765, to the commencement of our Revolutionary War, was but ten years. The Indians now beheld a new era, a new state of things, a new political division. A bloody contest had commenced between the *same* members of the *white* race; they saw their old *enemies*, the supporters of the British Crown, occupying the territorial position of their old *friends*, the French; whilst the people of the colonies, always their enemies, had added to their acts of atrocity against them, by making encroachments upon their great hunting ground, and the murder of many of their people, which excited new fears, and intensified their hatred toward them. Therefore, as all the traders among them were English, and in English interest, assuming the same position in regard to them, and exercising the same influence over them that the French traders had possessed ten years previous, they were led to believe that the British Government was the most likely to be of service to them, especially in the event of the colonies becoming a separate and independent power; and in case of their subjugation they knew they would be on the strong side, and have claims to the protection of the British Crown. Our Revolutionary Annals exhibit many of their acts as allies in a united cause.

The treaty of 1783, between Great Britain and at that time our independent States, by no means ended the conflict, or removed the cause of war between the *now*, and for the first time known among nations, "AMERICAN PEOPLE," and the Indian tribes, as during this era, commencing in 1775, a new and inexhaustible cause of war to them had arisen, producing, as it did, a long and bloody struggle! Adventurers from North Carolina and Virginia, pioneers of the white race, had penetrated their great hunting ground, always held sacred as a common *park* filled with game for the *use* of *all*, upon which no human being should have his home. These adventurers had, at the commencement of the war, already established themselves at Boonsborough, Lexington, Harrodsburgh. This invasion of the white man brought all the Indian tribes of the northwest to a general council, which was held at the principal town of the Shawanee nation, "Chillicothe," now marked on the map as "Old Town," above Xenia, Greene County. They decided that they had no alternative but to make frequent incursions at all seasons of the year, in such force as each tribe could furnish, and if possible destroy these settlements, and drive these aggressors from what they held to be their domain, their territory; that in addition to these efforts by land, the tribes most convenient to the upper parts of the Ohio River, moving out from the Muskingum, Kanawha, Scioto, and other streams in their canoes, should attack all the boats descending it containing families intending settlement.

From 1775 until 1791, this great struggle continued, at times with formidable force, always with bloody and destructive results.

We now arrive at the time 1791, when TECUMSEH, a mere lad as he was, began his active career!

The Indian had forever lost his great hunting ground!

The war in which they now engaged was their second crusade, and for the recovery of the boundary of the Ohio River. This they were promised by English traders, English officers, and every Indian interpreter representing the power of Great Britain at Malden, at the Maumee, at York; and this they greatly *hoped* for and *contended* for, (as I have mentioned,) from the defeat of Harmar and St. Clair, to the victory of Wayne, which closed their struggle and crushed their hopes for the time.

The treaty of Greenville, 1795, was signed.

Now it was that TECUMSEH commenced that

career which he ever afterward pursued. At St. Clair's defeat, and at the battle of the Rapids, he had established the character and gained the reputation of a YOUNG BRAVE of high promise. His ambition and genius caused him to take advantage of this; and from this day, accompanied by his brother, who a few years afterward became the renowned *Prophet,* visited all the tribes; learned all the traditions of every old chief whose tribe had at any time occupied land, or had their home near the ocean, and had been driven to the interior by the encroachments or insidious acts of the white race. They learned the history of their people; the unjust means always resorted to by the white man in obtaining their lands, and forcing them to remove from their long cherished homes. *This was the school in which* TECUMSEH *and the* PROPHET *were educated.* And from this time they exerted all their influence in opposition to every treaty made with us, and especially of every grant of land. In this they were ever consistent.

They thus commenced their third CRUSADE for the recovery of their old boundary, within which were the SEPULCHRES of their fathers, which, to them, was the HOLY SEPULCHRE, and their fondly cherished, beloved homes upon the Muskingum, the Tuscarawas, the beautiful Miamis of the South, the fertile and delightful borders of the Scioto, the LAND OF THEIR EARLY DAYS, the loss of which they always deeply mourned. This WAS THEIR "HOLY LAND."

I have described the council of Springfield in 1806, at which TECUMSEH gained the reputation of being the leading mind and great orator that shadowed forth the renowned leader in the war of 1812.

When hostilities between the British Government and the United States became threatening and the influence of British agents had become so great that the Indians commenced assembling in large bodies, as we have seen in 1811, TECUMSEH's prospects brightened. He was promised by all the British officers and agents at Malden, at York, at Montreal (all of which places he visited in person, in order that he should know, from the highest representatives of British power, what he could depend on), that in the event of a war between the two Governments, if he would bring a large force to their aid in the northwest, he might depend upon all the power of the King of Great Britain, all his warriors, all his ships which he would build on the great lakes, to reconquer for them all of the old northwestern territory, and never make peace with us until their OLD BOUNDARY OF THE OHIO RIVER should be secured to them forever.

This was the solemn promise to him and to his associate chiefs of all the tribes, in the summer of 1811; and these promises were repeated at the commencement of the war in 1812.

On the day previous to that on which the council of war, which I have heretofore mentioned, was held at Malden, TECUMSEH addressed to General Proctor a communication in writing, by the aid of his interpreter, whom he always kept with him after his forces had become formidable, it being important that all requests or orders from the British officer in chief command, should be clearly understood by him, as well as that his views and suggestions should be promptly and clearly understood by them.

This communication is dated at Amherstburg, September 18, 1813, and made

"In the name of the Indian chiefs and warriors

to Major General PROCTOR, as the representative of their GREAT FATHER, THE KING."

Among other declarations are these:

"*Father, listen to your children! You have them all before you.*"

"*When war was declared, our father stood up and gave us the tomahawk, and told us he was then ready to strike the Americans; that he wanted our assistance,* AND THAT HE WOULD CERTAINLY GET US OUR LANDS BACK WHICH THE AMERICANS HAD TAKEN FROM US."

"*Listen!* Our fleet has gone out; we know they have fought; we have heard the great guns," etc.

"*Listen! The Americans have not yet defeated us by land; neither are we sure they have done so by water,*" etc.

"*Father,* you have got the arms and ammunition which our GREAT FATHER sent to his red children. If you have an idea of going away, give them to us, and you may go, and welcome for us; our lives are in the hands of the GREAT SPIRIT. We are determined to defend our LANDS, and if it be HIS WILL, *we wish to leave our bones upon them!*"

Early in the spring of the year 1814, TECUMSEH

having passed away, all of his most devoted, subordinate chief warriors of the Shawanee, Delaware, Ottowa, Miami, and other powerful tribes left their encampments in Upper Canada, and passed down to Quebec, then the residence of the Governor General, for the purpose of conferring with him personally, and ascertaining from him, whom they knew to be the chief representative of the King, what they could depend on in the future, and what his views were in regard to a continuance of the war? They had been present with TECUMSEH at the beginning of the war, when the solemn promise had been given by Lieutenant General Prevost, as before noted. They now said to him:

"*Father, listen! Your red children want back their old boundary lines, that they may have the lands which belong to them;* AND THIS, FATHER, WHEN THE WAR BEGAN, YOU PROMISED TO GET FOR THEM."

"*Father, listen! The Americans are taking our lands from us every day. They have no hearts, father; they have* NO PITY *for us; they want to drive us beyond the setting sun.*"

The promises of General Proctor, at Malden, and of Sir George Prevost, Governor General of

Canada, at Montreal, representing the King and power of Great Britain, were made and broken! The treaty of Ghent was signed! No old boundary! Nothing secured to them!

The sepulchres of their fathers, and the sites of their beloved early homes, became the fields of the white man. Their HOLY SEPULCHRES and HOLY LAND were lost to them forever!

So ended their third and *last* crusade.

HIS HUMANITY.

TECUMSEH always claimed the honor of never permitting the death of a prisoner, and never permitting any greater sacrifice of life than was absolutely necessary to secure victory.

I met a large number of the principal warriors who convened at Greenville, and participated in making the treaty of peace of the 22nd July, 1814, many of whom had known Tecumseh from his youth, had been with him in the war of 1791 and the present war. They invariably testified to the correctness of this claim on his part, and said it "*was true;*" "*they knew it to be true.*"

In addition to this evidence, or in corroboration of it, a statement of an English officer of the highest reputation, as well as that of some American gentlemen who were present at the time, will be given.

When General Green Clay advanced with the Kentucky forces, from Fort Defiance to the relief of General Harrison, then besieged in Fort Meigs, General Harrison sent a despatch to him, General Clay, to land *eight hundred* men about two miles above, on the opposite shore from the Fort, march them down to where the enemy had their main battery, spike the guns, and then immediately re-enter their boats, and cross the river to the Fort. When the order was delivered, the noise of the rapids and dashing of the flotilla prevented Colonel Dudley, who was charged with this duty, from hearing the order distinctly, (as was alleged in extenuation by Dudley's friends, *though not admitted* by *General Harrison,* who by the reckless headlong movement that followed, unquestionably lost a brilliant advantage over his enemy,) and his men on landing, and carrying the battery, (which was on the bluff) without opposition, seeing a few Indians in the road before them, and a small number having fired on his advanced spies or rangers in the woods, with more impetuosity than caution, rapidly followed them. This was a stratagem of Tecumseh! His Indians appeared frightened, ran on before the Kentucky Volunteers; the road leading through a thick wood, on the high bank, along down in the direction of the old British Fort, (at which was one of the British camps,) keeping up a scattering fire, and running so as to lead on their enemy.

Tecumseh, in this manner, drew the whole regiment along between two columns or files of his warriors, posted on each side of the road on the ground, behind trees and logs. When all were within his ambuscade, on the instant that his signal was given, the columns closed upon Dudley's regiment; he was slain; all except about 150 men were prisoners. Tecumseh led them down to the old Fort, and delivered them to General Proctor, (the English officer in command,) immediately returning to the front with his warriors, ordering them with the promptitude and in the manner of a real commander.

Soon after he had regained his position opposite Fort Meigs, some cowardly, mean Indians (and every army has more or less of cowardly, mean, and cruel persons attached to it) commenced shooting from behind trees, and over the old walls at our men, and wounded several of them; although the officer on duty made every exertion to prevent it. He saw no other course than to send word to TECUMSEH, and accordingly despatched a courier on his fleetest horse for him. In a short time Tecumseh was seen dashing *at full speed* down the road with his sword drawn, and riding up to these miscreants, with the appearance of the greatest rage, struck them with his greatest force over the head and shoulders, with the flat of his sword, exclaiming: "*Are there no men here?*" The English officer informing me of this incident, said, "*He was the maddest looking man I ever saw*"—"*his eyes shot fire*"—"*he was terrible.*" The vile Indians vanished, and were not seen afterwards.

Many of the subordinate officers of the British army, who had served at Malden, Detroit, at the siege of Fort Meigs, and made prisoners of war at the battle of the Thames, were of the best English families—always gentlemen. They were courteous to us at Detroit. We were kind and courteous to them, when their turn came and arrived as prisoners at Cincinnati. From some of them I obtained important facts.

Many persons have written and published sketches of the life, character, and appearance of this celebrated Indian chief. Some of these have been written by persons who evidently did not see or even have any certain knowledge of what they attempt to describe.

All persons who have been in our armies during war, especially in our thinly settled part of the country, (and the old officers of our revolutionary war said it was the same in their time,) know what reliance there is to be placed in what are termed "camp reports,"—flying reports. During our first campaign the newspapers were full of them.

Among the publications to which I refer, is "*Brown's views of the campaigns of the northwestern army,* 1814."

He says : " *Tecumseh's ruling maxim in war was to take no prisoners, and he strictly adhered to the sanguinary purposes of his soul. He neither gave or accepted quarters. Yet, paradoxical as it may seem, to prisoners made by other tribes he was attentive and humane.* Nay, in one instance he is said to *have buried his tomahawk in the head of a Chippeway chief, whom he found actively engaged massacreing some of Dudley's men after they had been made prisoners by the British and Indians.*"

Paradoxical truly! HE took no "*prisoners,*" when but a year previous he had taken six hundred and fifty of Dudley's regiment. He sank his tomahawk into the head of a Chippeway chief! No tomahawk was seen; no Chippeway chief was there. They were HIS OWN prisoners, not *British* and *Indian prisoners*. The British had all fled from their battery to their camp at the old Fort.

This is a specimen of history where the writer depends upon common or camp reports, or his own imagination for facts. Mr. Brown evidently wrote at home and from hearsay. He further states, that *in the first settlement of Kentucky, he* (Tecumseh), *was particularly active in sinking boats going down the Ohio, killing the passengers, etc. Made frequent incursions into Kentucky, where he would invariably murder some of the settlers, and escape with horses loaded with plunder, etc.*

Now instead of all this, TECUMSEH's first warlike act of any kind was his participation in the conflict known as Harmar's defeat, in October, 1791, when he was a mere lad of sixteen years of age, in which he lost a beloved brother, several years older than himself, who was shot down at his side; which so shocked him in consequence of the timidity or feelings of early youth, or that this was his first battle; that he was charged, and laughed at by some of the old warriors, as showing the "*white feather,*" as he ran off the field when his brother fell, instead of assisting them to carry him off. He, however, never wavered afterwards.

This last defeat of Harmar took place but a short distance from his birth place, his beloved early home. He was also in St. Clair's defeat about a year afterwards, in which he gained credit for himself. And at Wayne's battle of the Rapids of the Miami of the Lake, on the 20th of August, 1794, he distinguished himself for his gallantry, and gained the name and standing of a "*young brave.*"

This was the advent of TECUMSEH, as a participator in the affairs of his nation and race. And the idea that he had been one of the warriors that had "*made frequent incursions into Kentucky in the* "FIRST SETTLEMENT" of that State, been among those terrible savages, who had been "*active in seizing family boats going down the Ohio, killing the passengers, etc.*," was both anachronistic and fabulous, as the destruction of the family of Greathouse, the coadjutor of COLONEL CRESAP in the murder of the entire family of the celebrated LOGAN, the "MINGO CHIEF," "the friend of the white man," (whose home was on the beautiful high bank, about four miles below Steubenville, on the Virginia side of the river,) was among the last of these terrible acts, and this was done by Logan's avengers of blood, *of his own tribe*, when Tecumseh was yet a mere boy; and as for the incursions into Kentucky, they had ceased for many years.

All this would be rich and amusing, but for the fact that it is destructive of the truth of history. Mr. Brown, however, deserves credit for having killed off HIS Tecumseh at the place where the heroic warrior doubtless fell, the battle field of the "THAMES." He says on that occasion "*there was a kind of ferocious pleasure in contemplating the contour of his features, which was majestic even in death.*"

HIS DEATH.

On the return of the Kentucky Volunteers, who had participated in the battle of the THAMES, at least a dozen of them appeared strongly impressed with the belief that they had slain this great chieftain; but no one of them pretended to any certain knowledge of the fact. The description given by them of the personal appearance of the warrior whom they claimed to have slain, did not, in any one instance, correspond with the personal appearance of TECUMSEH. The better informed gentlemen of that force, in the absence of all certainty, thought it as well to consider the Indian warrior, who confronted Colonel Richard M. Johnson, when he, at the head of his forlorn hope charged upon their line, and whom he certainly slew, to be this distinguished man. In this, however, they were as far from the truth as the others. Colonel Johnson informed me, and so he publicly stated, during the canvass of 1840, for the Vice Presidency, that he did not pretend to say that the Indian warrior referred to was TECUMSEH; he was not acquainted with his personal appearance; all that he knew was that a tall, athletic warrior confronted him, whom he slew, by discharging his pistol at him. The description given by him, of the appearance of this warrior, did not correspond. He was of too great a height; too large of stature, dark complexion, and *black* eyes! He had neither sword or pistols, only his gun, tomahawk and knife. *Of course he was not* TECUMSEH, as at all times after he became Brigadier General and Commander of the greatest Indian force, fully armed and organized, ever known in any war, under any one chieftain, was never in battle or in council without them; and his complexion, as I have stated, was light, and his eyes were *not* black, but a clear transparent hazel.

It was considered probable at the time, that he had been severely wounded, and borne from the field by his devoted and always attached corps of young chiefs, who were always with him, acting as aids, as runners, as messengers. There was no pursuit, the action lasting but a few minutes; the

English throwing down their arms as soon as Major Johnson's battalion had advanced upon them, which they did at full speed, breaking the line of battle, and thereby turning the flanks, and making it a matter of necessity for the Indians to retire. It was a mere charge, a single shock, and nearly all the Indian loss, and *our* loss was sustained by the charge of Colonel Johnson, with twenty valiant men, who with him at their head, as a forlorn hope, had voluntarily and with deadly loss, (in imitation of Wayne's tactics at the battle of the Rapids, in 1794, where General Harrison acted as one of his aids,) adopted this means to bring on the action.

There is one thing most certain, and that is, if TECUMSEH had been shot down, whether dead or alive, his body would have been borne from the field by his devoted warriors; nothing would have prevented them. The entire Indian force would have concentrated at the spot if necessary, and hundreds been slain before they would have permitted their great and beloved leader to have fallen into the hands of his enemies dead or alive. Neither the Greek or the Trojan, under the walls of Troy, ever contended with more devotion, more unyielding energy and pride for the bodies of their fallen heroes, than those attached, devoted warrior friends would have contended for him. He was mortally wounded, borne from the field after Proctor's forces had thrown down their arms. We thought it probable that his wounds might not prove mortal, that he would again in a few weeks or months re-appear at the head of his forces; but he did not, he had passed away.

When in the ensuing spring the delegation of his chief subordinate warriors went to Quebec, and had their interview with Sir George Prevost, as I have mentioned, Tecumseh's sister accompanied them. Sir George Prevost was Governor General of Canada. At the residence of the Governor General, Lady Prevost made to her many valuable presents, among them many emblems of "*Mourning*." This was the first, though not positive evidence of the death of the renowned chieftain, that I have ever met.

A large number of the warriors who had been with Tecumseh from the beginning of the war, up to the battle of the THAMES, and since that time had returned to their tribal homes, assembled at Greenville, the same place at which Wayne's treaty of the 3rd of August, 1795, was made, and entered into a treaty with our commissioners on the 22nd July, 1814. Among them were many who had known him from his youth; some of them had been in the habit of coming into Cincinnati with their interpreters every autumn after the treaty of 1795; bringing their furs, and obtaining their supplies. Frequently four to five hundred of each of the great tribes would annually do so, having their camps in the forest, where Dayton street now is, and at the head of Main street.

Among them were warriors who had during the war of 1791, taken some boys of respectable families, carried them home with them; afterwards ransomed, and growing up to be our most respectable and opulent citizens. Their old captors, bloody warriors as they were known to be in Harmar's and St. Clair's defeats, would make it a point to call and see them; and although the Indian never forgot a friend, or forgave an enemy; and when he reposed confidence in any one, and was not deceived, would ever be friendly with them. Yet with all this comparative intimacy and evident friendly feeling, we could never obtain from them any information as to Tecumseh's death; all appeared unwilling to admit that he was slain by the white man, that he fell at the "THAMES," or was dead; pride of feeling, pride of race, previous devotion to him, always prevented any explicit replies to questions on the subject. They were asked :

What has become of Tecumseh?

Raising the right hand to heaven, with an expression of the deepest sorrow,

"GONE."

Did you see him on the day of the battle?
"YES."

When did you see him the last time?

"*Just as the Americans came in sight, he with his young braves passed rapidly up and down the line, spoke to every old warrior; saw every one;* said ' BE BRAVES ;' '*stand firm; shoot certain.*'"

Did you hear after the battle that he was killed or badly wounded?

NO ANSWER.

In my records of that time, these lines close the description of the battle of the Thames.

Here the heroic Indian chieftain, the greatest of his race, doubtless fell. Yet no Indian that I have met, has admitted the fact; and no white man that I have seen, has with certainty known it.

INDEX

BABIE Col, 28
BATHURST Earl, 77 78
BAYNE Col, 86 Edward, 68
BERRY Taylor, 29
BOYD Col, 13
BROCK Gen, 45 49 50 62-64 70 72-74 76 78 82-83 85 116 123 127 Isaac, 65 74 Major General, 40
BROWN Mr, 148 150
BRUSH Col, 46 47 50 51 53 54 59 82 127 Henry, 45
CASS Col, 31 Lewis, 25
CHAMBERS James, 19 26
CLAIBORNE Hon Mr, 90
CLAY Gen, 144 Green, 144
CRESAP Col, 149
CROGHAN, 41
DALE Col, 90
DALIBA Lt, 73
DEARBORN Gen, 68 69 85 86
DIXON Capt, 41 72
DUDLEY Col, 144
ELLIOT, 10
ELLIOTT Col, 60 74
FINDLAY James, 25
GLADWIN, 132
GLEGG Major, 45 50 62 72 73 77
GOODMAN Sharon, 13
HANKS Lt, 42
HARDIN Gen, 93-95
HARMAR, 92 94-96 135 149
HARRISON Gen, 111 115 118 119 144 153 Gov, 14 William Henry, 13
HECKEWELDER Thomas, 19
HICKMAN Capt, 17
HIGHWAY John, 26

HULL Abraham F, 18 Brig Gen, 74 75 Capt, 18 29 GEN, 29 33-35 40 45 50 67 68 71-73 76 77 83 85 123-126 William, 17
INDIAN Logan, 149 150 Pontiac, 110 131 132 Tarfee, 98 Tecumseh, 11-13 36 38 74 87 88 90 91 96 99-102 110 111 113 115 116 118-123 131 135-140 143-156
JESUP Thomas S, 127
JOHNSON Col, 122 151 153 Major, 153 Richard M, 151
JOHNSTON John, 113
KEMPER Presley, 126
KENTON Gen, 95 97 100 Simon, 89
KYLE Capt, 43
LAWRENCE John, 26
MACDONNEL Col, 64 Major, 62
MANSFIELD Capt, 26 27 49 60 John F, 19
MARSHALL Chief Justice, 95
MAY Mr, 80
MCARTHUR Col, 30 31 40 75 Duncan, 25
MCFARLAND Stephen, 19
MCKEE 10 Capt, 60 74
MEIGS Gov, 17
MILLER Col, 18 James, 25
MUIR Major, 38 61
PATTERSON Col, 97 Robert, 89
PHILLIP, 110
PINCKNEY Capt, 85

PREVOST Gen, 127 George, 65 69 85 140 154 Lady, 154 Lt Gen, 68 74 77 140
PROCTOR 121 Col, 83 116 Gen, 118 119 122 123 138 140 145 Major Gen, 139
REYNOLDS Surgeon, 42
SAINTCLAIR, 135 Gen, 93
SAYRE Elias, 26

SHALER Judge, 23
SHORT Col, 41
SNELLING Capt, 31 41 Col, 41
TAYLOR GEN, 29 James, 29 45
VANHORNE Major, 33
WAYNE 135 153 Anthony, 19

www.ingramcontent.com/pod-product-compliance
Lightning Source LLC
Chambersburg PA
CBHW050641160426
43194CB00010B/1767